God's Scoundrels and Misfits

God's Scoundrels and Misfits

Lessons Learned and Opportunities Missed

MICHAEL BRASWELL
and
CLEMENS BARTOLLAS

Foreword by John Michael Helms

RESOURCE *Publications* • Eugene, Oregon

GOD'S SCOUNDRELS AND MISFITS
Lessons Learned and Opportunities Missed

Copyright © 2017 Michael Braswell and Clemens Bartollas. All rights reserved. Except for brief quotations in critical publications or reviews, no part of this book may be reproduced in any manner without prior written permission from the publisher. Write: Permissions, Wipf and Stock Publishers, 199 W. 8th Ave., Suite 3, Eugene, OR 97401.

Resource Publications
An Imprint of Wipf and Stock Publishers
199 W. 8th Ave., Suite 3
Eugene, OR 97401

www.wipfandstock.com

PAPERBACK ISBN: 978-1-4982-9736-3
HARDCOVER ISBN: 978-1-4982-9738-7
EBOOK ISBN: 978-1-4982-9737-0

Manufactured in the U.S.A.   SEPTEMBER 6, 2017

For Harold Bales, "The Southern Fried Preacher."
A friend to many with second chances for all

Contents

Foreword by John Michael Helms | ix

Introduction | xiii

1. When Being Good Isn't Enough | 1
    Matthew 19:16–26
    Acts 6–9
2. Favorite Son | 17
    2 Samuel: 13–18
    Luke 15:11–32
3. The Man Who Would Be King | 27
    1 Samuel 9:15–24
    1 King 3
    Joshua 1 and 24
4. A Mother's Ambition | 39
    Genesis 24–27
    Luke 1:46–55
    Luke 2:45–50
    Matthew 12:38–50
    John 19:26–27

CONTENTS

5. A Good Marriage Is Hard to Find | 51
   Genesis 29–31
   Ruth 1–4
   Mark 10:7–9

6. When Beauty Is Only Skin Deep | 61
   Judges 16
   The Book of Esther

7. A Liberated Woman | 72
   Luke 13:31–35; 23:1–12
   Matthew 14:1–12
   John 20:1–18

8. Making Choices at the Crossroads | 82
   Acts 5:1–9
   Acts 9:10–19
   Luke 17:11–19

9. Embracing Scars | 92
   The Book of Job
   Luke 10:25–37

10. The Freedom to Forgive | 101
    Matthew 18:21–35
    Acts 6:8
    Genesis 37

11. The Faithful One | 110
    Matthew 13:31–36
    Matthew 16
    Matthew 26:14–16

12. The Least Likely | 120
    Luke 19:1–10
    John 3:1–21
    Luke 18:9–14

Bibliography | 131

Foreword

EVERY PERSON IS BORN into a relational system. Each of us grows up in a family where a variety of interactions and relationships contribute to the person we become. Our personalities are also shaped by the relationships we have with our parents and siblings. Some family relational systems are healthy and others are not. Many of us experience some degree of dysfunction in our family system that has affected us in some way for better or worse. As far as family relationships and dynamics are concerned, biblical stories testify that indeed, there is nothing new under the sun.

In "God's Scoundrels and Misfits," the authors take the lives of approximately thirty biblical characters and retell them so we can see the big picture regarding their relationships, choices and consequences. When we step back and see the interactions in their family systems or the situations and relationships they were a part of, we are surprised at how often we see ourselves. An emotion or complication expressed in their story connects with one in our own experience as played out in personal, family, church or business settings. More than this, the authors also show how God was working in the lives of these characters, something they nor we are often aware of.

From Samson we learn that the moment our arrogance misplaces our dependence on God for our strength, we have set into motion our bondage to the enemy. From King David we learn that

Foreword

being heroes to others does not excuse us from being good parents. From Herodias we learn that revenge is not sweet and that eventually judgment awaits those who provoke God and His ways. From the rich young ruler we discover that we are often too tied to our possessions.

Through all of these experiences, the authors seek to show the reader how God sought to be redemptive by providing opportunities along the way for repentance through second chances that bubbled up from their sin and brokenness. This is no more clearly demonstrated than in the stories of Mary Magdalene and of Saul who became Paul. Both embraced their second chances and as a result, their lives were transformed. Mary Magdalene went from being a widowed or divorced woman with serious emotional and psychological problems to being a woman who was healed by Jesus. Out of gratitude, she followed Jesus, along with other women, and provided him and the disciples with financial support. She was present at his crucifixion and encountered the risen Christ at the empty tomb. Paul went from hunting Christians down and putting them in jail, and in some cases having them killed, to preaching to Jews first, then to Gentiles, seeking to convert them to Christianity.

Unfortunately, many others passed on their second chance opportunities. Despite David constantly reaching out to his son, Absalom, Absalom's desire for his father's throne was greater than his desire for his father's affection. As a result, he experienced an untimely demise. The authors point out that Jesus would have also extended a second chance to Judas as he did to Peter. What Peter embraced, Judas despaired of, choosing to hang himself rather than ask forgiveness for what he had done.

Some of these stories might be familiar to you while you may have never heard of others. Either way, you will find yourself identifying with many of the characters and some of their flaws, because we all have them. In a sense, that's what makes us human.

I have known one of the author's family for many years. Like his father before him, he places great emphasis on truths found in biblical stories to engage in relationships with others as well as in making life decisions. I have also come to understand that both the authors are university professors who care much more about the relationships they have had with their students than with any awards or writing accomplishments they have enjoyed. A number of their students have followed in their wake and are now professors and teachers as well.

None of us come from perfect families. We all have our problems to one extent or another. The authors do an excellent job of comparing and contrasting these biblical characters in order to show us the difference that God makes when we respond to the second chances given to us through His grace. The father of one of the authors was a jeweler who could assess a gemstone to see if it was flawless or worthless. Jesus is what makes the difference between our being a flawed gemstone of no value or a precious gemstone of inestimable worth. Throughout this book, the authors show how God can take all kinds of flaws in our lives and restore them so that they are not only beautiful, but also useful to Him as we serve others in this world.

John Michael Helms, DMin
Author of "Hoping Liberia: Civil War Stories from Africa's First Republic."
www.johnmichaelhelms.org

Introduction

FROM THE ANCIENT DAYS of oral traditions to classic and modern literature, stories are central to our existence. For better or worse, they inform us about the values of our times and often remind us of what virtues we have lost. As in Biblical times, our stories are both personal and tribal whether our tribe is viewed through the lens of our nation, race, region or religion. The stories of our lives embody our hopes and dreams as well as our fears and prejudice. Stories feed our imagination with color and texture, illuminating big, timeless truths. Yet, particularly in our personal stories, they may also hide the darker, more nuanced side of who we pretend to be as opposed to who we really are. Our stories reveal that we, like others before us, have at times been both hero and villain, victim and offender. Perhaps, our crimes are not about breaking the law of the land, but are instead, crimes of the heart. We heroes and villains live our existence through our stories in the nooks and the crannies of our relationships with each other and the great Mystery we encounter throughout our lives.

The Bible is the "big story" that reveals to us as it did to the people who are found in its mosaic, choices and consequences—who we are and who we can become. We often think it is in our nature as human beings to seek out God or gods to bring order and meaning to our existence. Abraham Joshua Heschel maintains that throughout history the Bible tells us otherwise. It is God in

INTRODUCTION

search of us. Sometimes we may find ourselves in the shallow end of history's pool, reading and even memorizing scripture—looking for easy answers that reinforce our own ideas about right and wrong. As we venture deeper into its mysteries, the stories of the Bible may convict us more than comfort us. No matter how much or how little prosperity comes to us, adversity is often just a step behind. An insurance ad once encouraged us to own a "piece of the rock" when what we really yearn for is "peace in the Rock." The Bible is the story of "real" life, not the alternative and virtual life of the internet and social media. It is the story of humanity's confounding contradictions that make us who we are. We are all victims and criminals of the heart, alternating between hope and despair. From the horror of the holocaust to the stranger who sacrifices his or her own life to save another, we struggle, each in his or her own way, with the forbidden fruit we have eaten as we seek redemption.

We are inclined to see Biblical personalities in black or white—good or evil. David is good, King Saul and Goliath are evil. In keeping with our modern penchant for bigger than life caped crusaders like Batman, Superman and the like, we tend to see heroes like David as monolithic Superheroes—the only thing missing is his cape. A deeper reading of stories in the Bible reveal that much as in modern life, the heroes found there had flaws, sometimes fatal ones that colored their perceptions of the world around them just it does with us in our time. Yes, David slew the giant, Goliath, and kept one step ahead of King Saul who plotted to destroy him. David also arranged for his loyal Captain, Uriah the Hittite, to be killed so he could have his wife, Bathsheba. There were also giants like John the Baptist who baptized Jesus and declared him to be the long-awaited Messiah, but later when he faced his own execution, experienced doubt and sent messengers to Jesus to ask him "if he was the one?" Who can forget Peter "the rock" denying Christ three times or Paul, perhaps the greatest of evangelists, who before he became Paul, was Saul, an enthusiastic advocate for the murder of Christians like Stephen.

Introduction

Some Biblical characters made the most of their second chances while others squandered their opportunities. For example, the wise young ruler, Solomon, eventually became a corrupt and greedy King. The proud, young peacock, Joseph, on the other hand, embraced the challenges of captivity and became a prominent ruler in Egypt, forgiving his brothers for selling him into slavery. The prodigal son repented and came home to his father's delight while his elder brother smoldered with resentment. Then there was Peter, the one who denied Christ, who repented and remained faithful, becoming the rock of the early church that he was intended to be. And of course, second chances and missed opportunities were not only the business of persons, they also applied to tribes, cultures and countries back then just as they do now. Prophets of old proclaimed the will of God and warned the wayward of the consequences that were to come if they didn't change. Often, they didn't. After floods and other natural forms of disaster as well as enslavement and exile occurred, those who repented were restored.

The choices and challenges that faced both major and minor personalities as well as nations in Biblical times are the same ones that face us in today's world. Some of us like the widow with her mite are willing to give all that we have while perhaps, more of us are like the wealthy man who chose to build bigger barns and storehouses so that he could eat and drink and be merry. The widow had a big heart and the wealthy man had a large bank account. Which did Jesus honor? Do we have issues with how big our bank accounts, homes and churches are as a measure of our worth as opposed to how big and sacrificial our hearts are? There is also a turning away from God collectively. Communities, cultures and nations often attempt to preempt Jesus' teachings and commandments with more self-serving, nationalistic and prosperity based versions of religion. What held true for Israel, holds true for our culture and nation as well. No matter what the context—personal, communal or cultural, we have all missed the opportunities and blessings that God offers and need all of the second chances we can get.

INTRODUCTION

The twelve chapters in this book are written to illustrate the different challenges that individuals and families face in today's world that persons in Biblical times also struggled with. The times may change, but the lessons often remain the same. Each chapter will include examples of Biblical characters and communities who made the most of their second chances and those who missed their opportunities. We will examine how their choices and the consequences that followed reflect our own life situations and outcomes. A series of questions will be provided at the end of each chapter for personal reflection and small group discussion.

1

When Being Good Isn't Enough
Matthew 19:16–26
Acts 6–9

> "Nothing is so easy as to deceive one's self."
> DEMOSTHENES

> "There are two kinds of criminals:
> those who get caught and the rest of the human race."
> CHARLES COLSON

> "The wonderful thing about saints is that they were human. They lost their tempers, got hungry, scolded God, were egotistical or testy or impatient in their turns, made mistakes and regretted them. Still they went on doggedly blundering toward heaven."
> PHYLLIS MCGINLEY

> "It is very hard to be simple enough to be good."
> RALPH WALDO EMERSON

FROM AN EARLY AGE we were taught to be good boys and girls, seen more than heard. Being good was being helpful, following the rules, and becoming a useful and responsible citizen. Once in school, being good often morphed into "making good grades." Peer pressure added the importance of being accepted and even to some extent, becoming popular in an ever-expanding definition of what it meant to be good. Measuring our young selves against the grades and social skills of others increasingly became a challenge—sometimes an overwhelming challenge that too often led to insecurity and anxiety concerning whether we were "good enough." It wasn't enough for us to compete with ourselves, to be the best we could be. Socially and academically our worth was often measured against what our older brothers and sisters did as well as our peers in school and the neighborhood. In our modern world of evolving technology with such things as smart phones, the internet and "selfies," the challenge of finding balance and stability in our lives seems to have become exponentially more demanding and frustrating.

In church, we learned early on that "Jesus loved all the little children—red and yellow, black and white." We sang songs, were taught Bible stories, learned the Ten Commandments and at various ages, came to experience the love and grace of Jesus. Sometimes bored, other times amazed, we listened to preachers and teachers tell us about sin and grace and about how we should live our lives as followers of Christ.

We live in a country and religious culture that extols the virtues of personal responsibility, moral behavior, hard work and helping those less fortunate than ourselves. Most of us have been taught that if we work hard and save our money, live an ethical life, give our tithe and help those who are suffering, we will have a good and satisfying life. And if we accept Jesus Christ as our personal Savior, our good life will continue on into the hereafter. Even if one is not religious, "only in America" resonates with promise and hope for a better life, a life that offers a motivated person the chance to rise to great heights of success. Perhaps, that is why so many disenfranchised individuals and families from around the world try to get to America any way they can.

Such thinking sounds simple and straightforward enough. If we Christians faithfully follow the commandments and instructions of Jesus, all will for the most part, be well. Of course, talking the talk and walking the walk are two different realities. Accepting personal responsibility for our actions and learning from our poor choices are important in our life's journey as is taking care of our family and close friends and even others in need on occasion. Still, it is easy enough for us to deceive ourselves into thinking that is enough. Jesus tells us that our responsibility encompasses more than that. "I was a stranger and you took me in. I was hungry and you fed me. I was naked and you clothed me. I was in prison and you visited me (Matt. 25:35–36)" speaks to a much broader and deeper obligation, one that we often turn away from. His words indicate that our charge to be compassionate and serve others moves well beyond our family and circle of friends. To make matters worse, he tells us to continue to forgive those who wrong and hurt us, essentially without limit and to pray for those who do us harm—who injure us physically, who try to destroy our good name. The tragedy in Charleston, South Carolina comes to mind where an angry and disturbed young white supremacist shot and killed black church members and their pastor who had invited him to join them in their weekly prayer meeting. Did they call for him to get the death penalty? Did they place armed guards at their church entrance? Did they arm themselves? No, although in a very real sense they did arm themselves in righteousness, embodying the essence of Christ's commandments as they forgave the assailant and prayed for his salvation. They didn't hold protest rallies at the police station. They held impromptu prayer meetings on the street corners of Charleston.

Hunger, homelessness, emotional distress, and hopelessness embodied the instructions Jesus gave us—to serve the least among us who are often the least like us politically, religiously, racially and ethnically. How can we feed the hungry? There are so many human beings in distress at home and abroad that it seems overwhelming to even think about such a feat. Mother Teresa exhorts us toward the "small way of doing things." Not big plans and campaigns, but to begin where we are with what we have. Louis Evely tells us that the only way for God to give bread to those who don't have it is for us to give them ours. The small boy with his inadequate and insignificant meal of a few fish and several loaves of bread through the blessing of Jesus fed five thousand people. He wasn't practical like the adults surrounding him, primarily concerned with feeding themselves and their own. He was too young and inexperienced for such practical considerations. He didn't offer a portion of what he had to Jesus. He offered it "all." And this is where we come to the story of "the rich young ruler."

THE RICH, YOUNG RULER

We don't really know why the young ruler ran up to Jesus as he and his disciples prepared to set out on a journey. Maybe as good as he was in the eyes of others, there was some slight doubt that gnawed within him and whispered during his evening prayers that still, he wasn't quite good enough. Or perhaps the young man of means had checked off all the boxes his religious tradition required and wanted to make sure all the t's were crossed and i's were dotted. Whatever his reasons, he asked the question: "Good Teacher, what "good deed" must I do to have eternal life?"

Good deed, indeed. Jesus' first admonished him with the question, "Why do you call me good? No one is good, but God alone" (Luke 18:19). And then Jesus checked off the commandments, one after the other to which the young ruler replied in earnest that he had kept the commandments since he was a boy. Jesus looked into the young man's heart and was moved by what he saw. The scriptures tell us that Jesus loved him—loved the effort he had made in keeping the commandments, loved his willingness to come and ask if there was something more for him to do, loved him in spite of what would come next.

It must have been with a hint of love and sadness in his eyes that Jesus gave the wealthy, young ruler the piece of the puzzle that he had until now, missed. Jesus replied that the only thing left for him to do was to sell all that he owned, give the money to the poor and follow Jesus. The shock of Jesus' requirement must have left the young ruler speechless. We are told that he went away grieving.

As the young man disappeared down the street, Jesus turned to his astounded disciples and informed them that it was nearly impossible for a rich person to get into heaven. The looks on their confused faces said it all: "If someone who was as good as the young ruler was couldn't be saved, what hope was there for them?" Perhaps, Jesus offered them a knowing smile when he told them that for "mortals it was impossible, but with God all things were possible."

The young ruler who came to Jesus has in some instances, been portrayed as selfish and self-important. Nothing could be further from the truth. He is, in fact, a better person than many of us. Why? First, he seeks Jesus out and kneels before him, reverently acknowledging his authority. He didn't avoid Jesus, going about his daily routine while looking over his shoulder, hoping he and the Master didn't cross paths—hoping he wouldn't have to change anything in his successful life. Second, when Jesus checked off the commandments that should be kept, commandments that few, if any of us could consistently keep in total, the young ruler replied, "Teacher I have kept these since my youth." It is at that point we are told that "Jesus, looking at him loved him . . . " When Jesus saw the young ruler's heart, what a powerful and compassionate moment that was. With all his riches and status, the young man's virtue was both apparent and consistent. Still, there was one thing left that troubled the young ruler. He at the very least, sensed that as good as he was, there must be something else—some other virtuous act that he needed to complete in order to quiet the uncertainty he felt in the deepest part of who he was. He hoped Jesus would tell him what it was. Perhaps, it was a new commandment, one that he could follow with the assurance that eternal life would be his.

ONE MORE THING

With love and compassion in his eyes, he looked at the eager, but troubled young man and told him that to complete the circle of his virtue, he did, indeed, need to do one more thing. Jesus said to him, "You lack one thing; go, sell what you own, and give the money to the poor, and you will have treasure in heaven; then come, follow me" (Matt. 19:21). We are told that when the young man heard what Jesus told him, he was shocked and went away full of grief because he had many possessions. Who among us would have done differently? The young man didn't arise indignantly and leave in a huff. His shock and grief were genuine and came from the same source—his possessions and perhaps, his reputation—all that he had worked for his whole life. Keeping the commandments had required much sacrifice—but not everything.

What would we have done in the young ruler's place? What more would we be willing to give up?

Compared to most of the world, we live in Disneyland. To some degree, the least of us economically speaking, would be considered very well off in most parts of our starving, strife-torn world. Like the young ruler, we have worked hard for what we have, whatever it amounts to, and we have tried to live good lives and follow Jesus—at least part of the time. Maybe, we even tithe. Maybe, we even exceed our tithe and are known to be generous with our time and money to charities and individuals in need. And yes, we do want eternal life. Can't we have both? Can't we keep our possessions and use them for good and have eternal life? Perhaps. Perhaps, not. What is the essential point Jesus is making? As painful to us as it was to the young man, His point is clear: "Nothing can come before me—not wealth, health, reputation or even family." We want to look away when we read the words in Job 1:21, "The Lord gives and the Lord takes away. Blessed be the name of the Lord."

What lies ahead requires us to leave the past behind. Easier said than done. Jesus tells us as he did his disciples to travel light, walk in faith. While you will have "dark nights of the soul," don't let doubt stop you. He is the map and the Holy Spirit is our tour guide. The words we need to speak will be given to us as well as whatever provision we need. We won't travel first class and the road will be rough at times. The big thing is we will not be alone. No matter what happens, we will not be alone—even when we feel alone. He will be with us.

So the rich, young ruler like we often do, missed his opportunity to change. He couldn't quite let go. Like you and me, he wanted his treasure both in the world and in heaven. He left grieving, but in some sense, relieved that he could keep what he had. Or could he? There are no guarantees. The road will still be rough at times and death will still come to him as it does to each of us, requiring that we leave whatever we have in this world behind. The good news is that we serve a God of second chances and of course, we need all the second chances we can receive.

FROM SAUL TO PAUL

Saul was an "up-and-comer", passionate, bright and dedicated to defending the church. He was from the tribe of Benjamin, a Pharisee and a Roman citizen as well. It is not surprising given his zeal in persecuting the early Christians that he was from a devout Jewish family. Saul was from the city of Tarsus, well-known as a center for trade and learning on the Mediterranean coast.

As a young man, he studied under Gamaliel, a highly esteemed rabbi, in Jerusalem. Being a student in such an environment and evidenced by his subsequent eloquence in expressing himself, Saul would have been rigorously immersed in the classics of his day—philosophy, ethics, theology and literature.

Saul was a true believer. Driven by religious and personal ambition, he was determined to stamp out the heresy that the early Christians represented—a heresy that threatened the established religious order and authority of Judaism. In Galatians 1:13–14, he later wrote, "You have heard, no doubt, of my earlier life in Judaism. I was violently persecuting the church of God and was trying to destroy it. I advanced in Judaism beyond many among my people of the same age, for I was far more zealous for the traditions of my ancestors." And zealous he was, for Saul was fully committed to ferreting out suspected Christian heretics wherever he could find them. After rounding them up, his hapless victims were submitted to a kind of inquisition where they could choose to either deny their new-found faith or face being sent to prison or worse.

And then came Stephen who may have had more in common with Saul than we typically realize, except that his passion and zeal was to proclaim rather than suppress the "good news" of the risen Christ. Brought before the high priest on trumped up charges, he was asked, "Are these things so?" Stephen's response started out well enough in describing the historical relationship between the Israelites and God, but the more he talked, the more animated he became. Stephen couldn't help himself. Maybe it was the pent-up frustration and anger pouring out over how the religious authorities neglected the widows and others who were poor or perhaps, it was the fire of the Holy Spirit speaking through him. Whatever it was, it wasn't pretty. Red-faced and sweating, if looks could kill, Stephen would have never been able to finish his speech. He concluded his rousing finish by saying "You stiff-necked people, uncircumcised in heart and ears, you are forever opposing the Holy Spirit, just as your ancestors used to do. Which of the prophets did your ancestors not persecute? They killed those who fore-told the coming of the Righteous One, and now you have become his betrayers and murderers. You are ones that received the law as ordained by angels, and yet you have not kept it" (Acts 7:51–53). After telling his audience that they and their fathers before them were a hard-hearted and hard-headed lot who had rebelled against and persecuted God's prophets, he topped things off by accusing them of betraying and murdering the very person who was sent to be their Messiah. That was it. We are told that Stephen's listeners became a frenzied mob, gnashing their teeth and dragging Stephen away to be stoned. So much for the law and due process.

Of course, stoning a man in his prime took a while so they needed someone to watch over their cloaks and belongings. No need to risk their valuables being stolen while they were doing the work of the church. In one of life's many ironies, who was assigned that task but the true believing, fire-in-his-belly Saul.

In a very real sense, Saul witnessing the stoning of Stephen and especially when Stephen knelt and cried out, "Lord, do not hold this sin against them" as he drew his last breath, may well have been a prelude to Saul's life-changing experience on the road to Damascus. It was a scene Saul who was to become Paul, would never forget. How could he?

After the death of Stephen, Saul continued his high-octane hunt for Christian heretics. The Scriptures state, "But Saul was ravaging the church by entering house after house; dragging off both men and women, he committed them to prison" (Acts 8:3). The young fire-breathing Pharisee continued on his rampage, advocating the murder of Christ's disciples. At some point, he requested the high priests to provide him with letters to the synagogue at Damascus so he could look for men and women who followed the new way of Jesus. He intended to arrest them and bring them to Jerusalem to face justice. Receiving his letters of introduction, Saul set off for Damascus full of vim and vigor.

And then it happened and when it did, Saul didn't know what hit him.

Can you imagine being Saul? On your way to do what you fervently believe is God's Will in stamping out heretical threats to Israel's traditional religious values, you are struck blind, deaf and dumb. From out of nowhere, a light brighter than a thousand suns hits you squarely between the eyes. To make matters worse, when you regain some modicum of consciousness, a voice calls out to you not once but twice, "Saul, Saul, Why are you persecuting me?" The voice without a face, the voice that surrounds you and rings in your ears like the peal of church bells on Christmas morning is none other than Jesus of Nazareth. It would seem to be nothing less than pure insanity. Saul may have felt much the same. What we do know is that the fervor with which he had pursued the followers of the Nazarene became a fever that burned through his former purpose and transformed him into the person he was meant to become, the Apostle, Paul. Jesus informed Saul that he needed a few good men and Saul was to be one one them. The Christ that the grave couldn't hold wanted Saul, his chief persecutor, to become his chief defender and advocate. How crazy is that? Saul's brain must have been addled at the thought of it. He was blind for three days and had to be led like a child to Annanias who ministered to his needs and baptized him. When Saul awoke as Paul, the fire was still in his belly. He had turned on a dime from being the grim reaper to becoming the "good news" gladiator. (See Acts 9:1–6, 22:4–16, 26:9–18).

We can only imagine what Paul's fellow travelers felt like; they clearly heard the voice and the conversation between Saul and Jesus, but saw nothing. Perhaps, their initial instinct was to break and run for the hills, but after considering the power of what they had experienced, they decided to lead a dumbstruck and blind Saul to Damascus and do as they were told.

LESSONS LEARNED AND OPPORTUNITIES MISSED

Both the rich, young ruler and Paul were faced with a second chance Jesus offered them. One turned away and the other was transformed from Saul to Paul. One was asked to give all he possessed to the poor and follow Jesus, living as he and his disciples did in service to the poor and hopeless and spreading the "good news." The other was knocked senseless by the blinding light of a truth that unveiled the difference between what he thought he was doing as opposed to what he was really doing. In both cases, Jesus' invitation required a dramatic, immediate change in the course of their lives, not the gradual incremental change that most of us desire, if we are willing to accept any change at all.

One could surmise that the comparison between the rich, young ruler and the rabid Pharisee who relentlessly persecuted Christians isn't quite fair. While to some extent, such a point may hold some degree of merit, there are distinct and interesting similarities between the two. Both men were devout Jews who were intent on doing good and following their faith. Both were true believers and held in high esteem by their colleagues and communities. While their personalities and vocations may have been different, both men were faced with the same basic choice—follow or don't follow.

The young ruler lived a moral life and kept the commandments of his faith. As previously pointed out, the Scriptures indicate that when Jesus looked into his heart and saw the man that he was, he loved him. Jesus also saw the man he could be. Jesus saw what was keeping him from his full potential. The man Jesus saw was an extraordinary person, industrious, respected and wealthy and at such a young age—a man who was trying to balance his goodness with his wealth. Like us, he wanted to "have his cake and eat it too." And who can blame him? When we work hard, try to do the right thing, attempt to follow Christ, and as a result, are blessed with wealth which we are willing to share with the less fortunate, why shouldn't we be able to "eat some of our cake"? Perhaps, we can, but we may also be asked like the rich, young ruler was to give up all of our "cake" and eat and drink from the cup that Jesus offers us, a cup that binds us to his purposes. In other words, Jesus was essentially telling the good, young man that *nothing* can come between me and you. In the end, the young ruler couldn't quite do it. It is said that he grieved over his choice not to follow Jesus, but as time passed, maybe as was stated previously, he was also a bit relieved. Maybe he could be content with going half-way. After all, half way was better than going none of way. Or is it?

After all, money and wealth can do a lot of good—feed the hungry, provide care for the sick, clothe the naked and house the homeless. Perhaps, we and the rich young ruler might also consider what it can't do. Money can't buy us more time which is the real currency of life. Our time is always short. Wealth can buy us fairweather friends and perhaps, a trophy spouse or two, but we find out who our real friends are when our money is gone and our time is short. Our money and possessions do not tell the real story of who we are. Our character and compassion is what defines us. What we have is much less important than who we are.

We should not be too quick to judge the choice the young ruler made lest we look into the mirror of our own choices on a much less dramatic scale. We often try to do the right thing—we really do. The trouble is, the more money we have, the more we are tempted to believe that there is no problem money can't solve. It is easy for us to forget that both our possessions and our time with them is "borrowed" not owned. The bad news is that our time is shorter than we think and the wealth of the world is more often than not, fool's gold. The "widow's mite" points toward what the rich, young ruler missed—that a generosity of spirit and sacrifice enjoys a wealth where "moth and rust doesn't corrupt."

Unlike the rich, young ruler, Paul never met Jesus until he was on the road to Damascus. He was full of enthusiasm for the task at hand and an educated and devout Pharisee intent on defending his faith. His elders and the chief priests admired and supported him in stamping out Christian heretics through punishment, imprisonment and even murder. Sure, he used violent means, but they were for a good purpose and when one is engaged in a "holy war," the means often justify the ends don't they? At least, that was what Paul and the religious authorities of his day believed. Before his conversion, Paul genuinely believed he "spoke the truth" and acted in ways to preserve the true faith, but he didn't "speak the truth in love" until after his conversion. After his conversion, Paul was different. Often hungry and scorned, whipped and beaten and on the run for his life, Paul limped along like Johnny Appleseed, planting the "good news" of Jesus Christ wherever he went. The light that had blinded him on the road to Damascus led him through hell and highwater as he stayed true to his mission. He stayed the course, kept his faith and finished his race.

It would be easy to conclude that since Paul's experience was so dramatic, he would be more likely to embrace his second chance than the rich, young ruler. That could be true, but so could the opposite conclusion. Imagine such an event happening to Paul in modern times, particularly given what is currently happening in the Middle East and around the world. Paul might be aggressively following his religion, purging his land of infidels and nonbelievers. One afternoon while driving the official church van with several of his colleagues to a nearby town where he had heard there were heretics witnessing to the faithful, he pulls his vehicle over to a rest stop. While checking his GPS to make sure he has the right directions, he is suddenly paralyzed by a blinding light. His head hurts, he can't see and he hears a voice. His colleagues can hear what is going on, but can't see what Paul sees. And the worst thing is that the person Paul can see and hear is turning his world upside down and sideways at the same time! Everything he had been taught and done was wrong. As good and devout as he had thought he was, he was the opposite of that. Can you imagine what his colleagues thought and how they might respond after such an event? Was it something we ate at "Bubba's Barbeque" in that backwater town we passed awhile back? Is Paul having an aneurism? He's been burning the candle at both ends lately; maybe he's having nervous breakdown. There's a hospital not far from here. Maybe they have a psychiatrist. We can't tell anyone what we just heard, especially the high priest and the elders. They might think we're crazy too. And anyway, it would be bad for our careers.

It would be a mistake to assume that since Paul's conversion experience was so dramatic and profound, that his transition from Saul to Paul was clear and straightforward. The radical change that occurred in Paul elicited a radical response from those he had held dear. We know that his parents cut off relations with him. It was a time of turmoil and grief as he left the love and support of his old life and began his new one. What we do know is that in the end, Paul accepted his second chance with a full-body embrace. Punch-drunk with the Holy Spirit and delirious beyond reason with what he had found, Paul did a 180 degree turn. He began preaching "for" the very thing he had previously been persecuting. It's not hard to guess the confusion and anger his previous supporters and advocates expressed concerning his sudden change. To them, Paul was a traitor—nothing less than a Benedict Arnold.

As soon as he recovered in Damascus, Paul immediately began to proclaim that Jesus was indeed, the Son of God. "All who heard him were amazed and said, 'Is not this the man who made havoc in Jerusalem among those who invoked this name? And has he not come here for the purpose of bringing them bound before the chief priests? (Acts 9:21)." A perplexed state of confusion among the people and priests quickly turned toward silencing Paul permanently. He went from being a hero of his faith to a traitor and a dangerous one at that—a person that needed to be stopped. The good news he was spreading was bad news for them.

Paul's basic personality didn't change. His heart did. He was still as single-minded as he had ever been and he could still hold a grudge, at least for a while. And he had his squabbles with the original disciples, especially where the Gentiles were concerned. Paul also had his dark nights. He writes, "I do not understand my own actions. For I do not do what I want, but I do the very thing I hate" (Rom. 7:15). No truer words have ever been spoken or written. Even when he couldn't go on, he went on. The point is that no matter how hard times got, no matter what the circumstances were, Paul never stopped—couldn't stop. He persevered.

As far as Paul was concerned, all were welcome to become Christ's "chosen people." He wrote in Galatians, "There is no longer Jew or Greek, there is no longer slave or free, there is no longer male and female; for all of you are one in Christ Jesus" (Gal. 3:28). Paul continued his journey into Christ with a wide-eyed enthusiasm that remained unabated no matter the circumstances to the end of his days. The gospel, grace and love were his constant refrain. He didn't just preach it, he lived it. Perhaps, there is no one who made more of his second chance than Paul.

It is thought that Paul was finally beheaded just outside of Rome. He was not one to waste an opportunity. Wearing the miles he had traveled on his weather-worn face and bearing the scars he had endured for his beloved's sake, one can imagine Paul telling his executioners about Jesus as the axe fell. Paul had finished his race. It was time to go home.

QUESTIONS FOR REFLECTION AND DISCUSSION:

1. In what ways are we like the rich, young ruler? There's an old saying that states, "You start out running your business, but your business ends up running you." Do we put too much stock in our possessions and whatever wealth we possess? Can you recall an insurance company who ran an ad on television that encouraged viewers to "own a piece of the rock?" Do we struggle with what has the greater importance in our lives—a piece of the rock or peace in the rock?

   From the outside, the rich, young ruler appeared for the most part, flawless, yet Jesus saw more deeply. What did Jesus see? What would Jesus see if he looked into our hearts?

   If Jesus appeared to us and asked us to do what he asked of the rich, young ruler, what would we do?

2. What are some ways we can learn and remember the lessons the rich, young ruler failed to learn? What role does self-deception play in our lives as we try to "be in the world, but not of it"?

3. Given the angry mob's reaction to Stephen telling them the harsh truth about who they really were as opposed who they pretended to be, how would you or I like being publicly reminded and reprimanded regarding our own family's hypocrisy and sin?

4. Stephen's "imitation of Christ" as he lay dying in asking that his murder not be held against his killers is a profound and humbling lesson. Typically, we want it both ways. When we have been harmed or betrayed, we often prefer the retribution of the Old Testament. Conversely, when we have betrayed or hurt someone, we yearn for a dose of New Testament forgiveness. In keeping with Stephen's example, how does it feel when we have betrayed someone and deserved a response of anger and rejection, but instead received the embrace and grace of forgiveness? How should it transform us?

5. Paul was passionate and determined regarding what he believed. His dedication to guarding his religion against the corruption of outside influences was single-minded and both religious and political. Are we more passionate concerning political or religious issues? Do we often tend to be more concerned with our material security or our spiritual security? What are the dangers of comingling them?

   What lessons can we learn from Paul's radical transformation? His highs and lows? His personal sacrifice?

6. Which one, the rich young ruler or Paul, had the most difficult choice to make? Things are not always what they seem. Sometimes, the more dramatic, in-your-face experience seems to require the more straight-forward choice, yet the less dramatic, more subtle circumstance can also offer the trickier and more seductive option in what we choose to do.

   A case can be made for either Paul or the rich, young ruler regarding which was the more difficult choice to make. Both required sacrifice and radical change. How do you think you would fare in either case?

2

Favorite Son

2 Samuel: 13–18
Luke 15:11–32

> "As the twig is bent the tree inclines."
> — VIRGIL

> "Nobody's family can hang out the sign 'Nothing the matter here.'"
> — CHINESE PROVERB

> "The central problem is that we do not know how to think, how to pray, how to cry, how to resist the deceptions of too many persuaders."
> — ABRAHAM JOSHUA HESCHEL

WE ALL HAVE OUR favorites. Over the course of a lifetime's worth of experiences, we cultivate preferred tastes for such things as food, fashion, entertainment and perhaps most of all, in relationships.

The warmth of a smile, the quirky turn of a head or laughter that comes from somewhere deep within that draws you closer to its source are examples of gestures and qualities which pull us into friendships and romantic intrigue alike. When our senses fully engage the person who attracts us in ways no other person can, romantic interest often follows eventually giving way to a new kind of favorite, a taste, even if just a sample, of a love that passes our understanding. Marriage is often the result and as much as we may come to love our spouse, we often find that the children born of that union offer us another experience of cherishing someone who is a part of us more than we love ourselves.

Loving someone else more than ourselves is the good and perhaps, most intimate part of our relationship with our favorite persons—the ones we love the most. As every coin has two sides, so do relationships. We don't just love our children, we also often spoil and enable them. In contemporary society, we hear a lot about self-esteem where everyone is a winner and not so much about self-respect where everyone is responsible for his or her actions—where the consequences of mistakes and losing are acknowledged and learned from. Unfortunately, self-esteem can too easily create a false sense of self-pride and a vain illusion that tends not to end well. It is worth noting that prisons are filled with offenders who have self-esteem and remember with a certain amount of pride about successful criminal endeavors which of course, don't include the crimes that put them in prison. Those who learn self-respect can change and become useful citizens while those who don't are apt to return time and again to prison.

The birth order of our children may also play a role with who becomes a favorite son or daughter. Oldest children tend to have higher expectations placed upon them. For better and worse, oldest children often hold the top position of the sibling pecking order, even at times being seen by their brothers and sisters as little more than a "junior parent." Middle children can come to feel like they are caught in the middle. They may be expected to both lead and follow, adapting as they go. Unlike the oldest and youngest, they may also feel left out. While an only child may mature more quickly into a little adult since they have their parents' full attention, the youngest child often has the strongest emotional bond with his or her parents. The last child often receives the most attention and affection which can end up being as much a burden as it is a benefit.

This chapter focuses on two classic examples of a father's favorite son. The prodigal son was the youngest. While his older brother worked, he apparently played. His desire was to head toward the bright lights of the big city. He wanted to go where the action was—where the beautiful and cool people hung out. We don't know whether the prodigal son was handsome or not, but we can guess then as now, if one has the money to spend, many of his new-found friends will find him quite handsome and clever.

In Absalom's case, we know that he was handsome and charismatic, a real charmer with the carefully styled flowing hair of a rock star and the ambition to match.

ABSALOM AND THE CRACKED MIRROR

Absalom seems to have had the good looks to go along with his fabled mane of hair. He also possessed a kind of athletic charisma which in spite of his tendencies toward impulsiveness, drew people to him. He was a charmer of sorts. Perhaps, he never met a stranger and in the moment he met with someone, working class or privileged, he made them feel special. Had Absalom lived in our time, we could imagine him roaring down the highway in a European convertible with his entourage, hair in a fashionable pony-tail and wearing expensive sunglasses as he headed toward some exclusive event like the Canne film festival.

Like his father before him, Absalom was a born leader. Unlike his father, he had not grown up as a shepherd boy, the runt of his family's litter. Instead, he had been a child of privilege, a prince and son of his father, King David. There were no sheep for him to watch over and protect from predators in the king's palace. Instead, Absalom was the protected one. In a sense, he was a sheep who wanted to be a lion. And who was there to tell him otherwise? He was both the apple of his father's eye and at times, the bane of his father's existence. Spoiling him on the one hand and demanding that he change his ways on the other, did little to instill discipline or integrity in Absalom.

Absalom was clever enough to exact his revenge on his half-brother, Ammon, who had raped his sister, Tamar, and left her dishonored and in a state of despair. He was patient, waiting two years to set the trap by inviting his brothers to a social gathering where his servants plied his guests with wine. When they were intoxicated, Absalom instructed his servants to kill Ammon. When the deed was done, he high-tailed it to Geshur to escape justice and his father's wrath. As, perhaps, had happened many times before, David was both furious at his son's actions and missed his presence at the same time. Three years later, Absalom was allowed to return, but was not allowed to see his father, the King. When Joab didn't respond to his request to intervene with David on his behalf, Absalom's impulsiveness once again got the better of him and he ordered his servants to set fire to Joab's hay field. In spite of it all, in time David allowed his beloved son to return to his good graces. Absalom had his second chance, one of many second chances his father had given him.

Like other handsome men and beautiful women of privilege before him, when Absalom looked into a mirror he reveled in his attributes. With the practiced eye of a narcissist he admired himself and felt confident in his ambition with little or no thought regarding how his actions might affect others. Absalom did not realize that he was looking into a cracked mirror like those found in modern day carnivals, one that exaggerated and fed the grandiose perceptions of what he wanted to see—of what he looked like on the outside. What he didn't see or have any insight into was what was on the inside. His intoxicating countenance and smile masked a dark and self-absorbed heart.

Throughout his life Absalom was more familiar with second chances than with consequences. Movie-star handsome, a big personality and a life of unlimited privilege can prove to be a lethal combination. Absalom could not leave good enough alone. He wanted more. David wanted his son. Absalom wanted his father's kingdom. So he worked the crowd and built up his public image with magnificent chariots and fifty men running before him. Pretending to be king-like, in the eyes of many he was king enough. In the end, Absalom entered Jerusalem victoriously, but for him, the end had not yet come. The battle of relationships between father and son inevitably came down to a battle of men—between the pretender to the throne and the old King who wasn't sure he wanted it anymore.

Even on the eve of the crucial and deciding battle between Absalom and David's armies, David seemed as or more concerned about the safety of his son, the usurper, than his own. He wanted to keep his throne, but at the expense of his son? Absalom apparently had no such concerns.

What must have annoyed David's three army commanders to the point of a seething if unspoken anger, was the old king's demand that they not harm Absalom if he fell into their clutches—the same Absalom that intended to take his father's throne and seemed more than willing to take his father's life.

Unfortunately for Absalom and his father, it was Joab who overtook Absalom as he was fleeing the field of battle. In one of life's more poignant ironies, the same magnificent hair that caused women to swoon and men to gush with admiration, trapped Absalom in the branches of an oak tree. His mule kept going, but he hung there, swinging back and forth. He must have seen Joab and his men approaching. Who knows what went through Absalom's mind during those last, fleeting moments of his life? Was there fear and regret as he realized too late the error of his ways or did he, in fact, expect Joab to free him from the branches of the mighty oak and let him go? Who can say for certain? What we do know is that Absalom and David's stream of second chances had run dry. There would be no more opportunities for David to teach Absalom to be the son he yearned for nor Absalom to accept the responsibility for the mistakes he had made and learn from them. The tip of Joab's spear that pierced Absalom's heart also broke David's as the old King's lament was heard throughout his chambers, "O my son Absalom—my son, my son Absalom—if only I had died in your place! O Absalom my son, my son (2 Samuel 18:33)!"

THE PRODIGAL SON: WHEN THE LIGHTS WENT OUT

In some ways, the prodigal son and Absalom were alike. Both were apparently impulsive and self-indulgent, more interested in doing what pleased them than doing what pleased their fathers. The fathers of both held great affection for their favorite and pampered sons. The prodigal son and Absalom felt entitled and were enabled by their families. Both had siblings who envied their favored status and resented what they got away with. Absalom and the prodigal son could both be headstrong and stubborn and apparently did not learn from the mistakes they made.

There were also marked differences between the two. While the prodigal son's father was obviously successful, he was not a King. As a result, the prodigal son seemed more interested in escaping the drudgery of farm life and hard work his brother and father endured than in replacing his father as head of the family. He was looking for a good time while Absalom was looking for a king's crown. There is also no indication that he held grudges or was a schemer and manipulator like Absalom or was motivated to use violent means to achieve what he wanted. Based upon the end results, we can safely assume that the prodigal son was not particularly charismatic or astute in managing his resources in the pursuit of what he saw as "the good life."

The prodigal son is more of an archetypal than a historical story. It is a story that is as much about how we raise our children today as it was about parenting in Biblical times. He didn't want to wait for his inheritance or even earn it through his own efforts. He saw it as his birthright—an entitlement—which, of course, it was. His older brother stayed and he left. We can see the younger brother riding out of town, his mules or camels laden with the riches his father had, though perhaps reluctantly, given him. We can imagine what kinds of thoughts were going through the young man's mind—"good riddance," "free at last," "big city, here I come" and so forth. He didn't worry about tomorrow. Why should he? He had never had to before. That was what his father and brother did. "Eat, drink and make merry," "live for today," "don't worry, be happy"—that's all that mattered.

In a real sense, the prodigal son also saw a distorted reflection of himself when he looked in the mirror. He most likely saw a young man full of self-esteem and self-confidence being held back from the life he deserved by his father. Most of his life his role had been a favored one, one where he spent the money his father and brother had earned. In his mind, that's what special people do.

We aren't told how long it took him to squander his resources, but it may well have taken less time than we would imagine. As indicated previously, when one has plenty of money to spend and throw around, friends seem to spring up from everywhere to stroke one's ego. Words like genius, brilliant and handsome along with other effusive expressions of adoration typically abound. What a life! Until the day it all comes to an end—until the day you no longer feast with the beautiful people, but instead compete with the swine for their slop. From excess and extravagance to poverty and despair, a timeless lesson that has played itself out since human beings roamed the earth beginning with Adam and Eve.

LESSONS LEARNED AND OPPORTUNITIES MISSED

The prodigal son squandered his inheritance and found himself knee-deep in the muck of a pig pen scrambling for scraps from the dinner table of the master he served. The crows had come home to roost. He was reaping the harvest he had sewn. What went around had come around. The ghosts of his excess and irresponsibility had come back to haunt him. Like many of us have experienced in our own lives, the prodigal son found out that pride and arrogance do, indeed, go before the fall.

While he may have been something of a spoiled brat, unlike Absalom, he was not a narcissist. He was capable of accepting some measure of responsibility for his mistakes. Crying tears of despair among the swine, the prodigal son realized two things through honest self-appraisal. Given the choices he had made and the way he had behaved, he was not worthy to be called his father's son. He also knew that his father was a good man, a man who took care of the needs of even the lowliest who served him. In other words, through confessing the error of his ways and feeling genuine remorse for his actions, he could imagine the possibility of redemption—he could find a glimmer of hope in the midst of his hopelessness.

What about Absalom? What insights did he gain when his second chance came and he was restored to his father's good graces after returning from his exile? Apparently none. There is no evidence that he saw or acknowledged the error of his ways. Instead, it seems that Absalom's conclusions were different. First, once his father received him, like all the times before, all was forgiven; and second, he could continue pursuing what he perceived to be his destiny—his father's crown. With no confession, at least internally, and no remorse, for Absalom, there was no opportunity for redemption. Did Absalom love his father? Who can say for sure? It is clear that unlike the prodigal son, he didn't respect him. There is also little doubt that he knew how to play David—what buttons to push to get what he wanted.

What about the fathers, what role did they play in second chances taken and opportunities missed by their respective sons?

David may have been King of Israel, but it isn't clear that he was in charge of his family. While no father is perfect and we all make plenty of mistakes, the example David set for Absalom was far from ideal. There was Bathsheba and his other wives and concubines—and his children who were half-brothers and sisters to each other—all competing for his attention and affection. Then there was his favored son, Absalom, watching his father's ups and downs as he maneuvered and manipulated his way through the myriad of relationships with which he was engaged. Absalom would be well-acquainted with the stories of his father's glorious conquests on the field of battle. He would also be aware of David's inglorious conquests in the bedroom, including how he came to make Bathsheba one of his wives. It seems that Absalom inherited David's ambition and charisma, but not his heart for repentance.

We don't know much about the prodigal son's father. Only that he was a wealthy man who along with his elder brother worked hard for what he had achieved. More importantly, we understand from his errant son's words that he was also a good, just and merciful man.

The prodigal son's father not only yearned for his son to return come home, he waited faithfully down by the road, hoping for his son's return. David also yearned for his son's return, but unlike the prodigal's father, he didn't let Absalom eat the husks of his choices and wallow in the pigsty of his own making. And while the prodigal son's father waited down by the road, David withdrew into his palace. Maybe David was tired. It even seems that he would rather give up his kingdom than fight his son for it. The heart connection was also missing. He loved Absalom, but in light of Absalom's ambition and desire, it was a one-way street with no return lane. In spite of the prodigal son's rebellion and self-centeredness, he and his father had a relationship that David and Absalom didn't enjoy.

In more ways than one, we are all prodigal sons and daughters, at times rebelling against the better part of what we learned from our earthly parents as well as our heavenly father. Career ambitions, the lust for power and status and our insecurities can side-track the best of our intentions. We find ourselves on more than one occasion lost not only from ourselves, but from the very ones we love the most. Sometimes we have to run out of money and the world's answers before we can begin to find our way home. Confession and remorse leads us toward redemption, lessons we often have to practice daily. Like the prodigal son, our faith in the memory of the father who loves us, guides us back to the place we belong. Like the prodigal son, we ask our Father who waits for us down by the road for mercy. And he grants it because he is the father of second chances.

QUESTIONS FOR REFLECTION AND DISCUSSION:

1. We all have our favorites. Some like chocolate and others like vanilla ice cream. Some like to watch comedies while others prefer mysteries. Some of us like the noise and excitement of the city while others prefer the quiet and solitude of the park. How do you think we come to favor one thing or another, one type of person or another?

2. What do you think is the difference between self-esteem and self-respect? In today's world which one do you think is more of a priority with most parents in raising their children?

3. What role do you think physical attractiveness and status plays in how a person sees themselves? How others perceive them? How was it both an advantage and a stumbling block for Absalom?

4. What are some differences between the two fathers, David and the prodigal son's father, in how they raised their two sons. The outcomes for each son were different. What could each father have done differently that may have resulted in their son being more mature and responsible for their choices?

5. Contemporary parents are faced with the same challenges that parents in biblical times faced. For example, what about our children like the elder brother who worked hard and did the right thing only to see his less responsible younger brother get perhaps, the lions-share of attention and resources from doting parents? There can be a fine line between supporting and enabling one's child. What are some ways today's parents can strike the most effective balance?

3

The Man Who Would Be King

1 Samuel 9:15–24
1 King 3
Joshua 1 and 24

> "Beware of the chief seat, because it shifts."
> JEWISH PROVERB

> "You rulers on earth, fear the rulers in heaven."
> AESCHYLUS

> "A good leader takes a little more than his share of blame; a little less than his share of credit."
> ARNOLD H. GLASGOW

> "A genuine leader is not a searcher for consensus but a molder of consensus."
> MARTIN LUTHER KING JR.

God's Scoundrels and Misfits

It was a brutal time and they were at best, an unruly and unpredictable lot, leaders and their subjects alike. Samuel warned his people that Yahweh was the only king they needed—that the kings of the world were a dime a dozen, more in it for themselves than for the people they reigned over. All they had to do was look around and see that such kings tended to use their sons as cannon fodder, coerce their daughters to work as their servants, collect taxes to build palaces and when the need arose, take their livestock and crops by royal decree. Samuel's efforts fell on deaf ears. Kings were in fashion and besides, everyone else in the neighborhood had one. The Israelites like many of us today were inclined to become obsessed with "keeping up with the Joneses." They wanted a strong-man—someone they could see, a flesh-and-blood champion they could point to with pride.

From Biblical times to our present time, things haven't really changed that much. Kings, Presidents, Emperors, and Prime Ministers and all other form of potentates have throughout history reigned for a time on earth. They ruled over kingdoms of the world with all of the world's prospects and promises. Pomp and circumstance, parades of spectacle and magnificent statues and edifices all trumpeted the myth of their immortality. While some even claimed to be gods, many of them wanted to be treated as such. There have been leaders who though scarred by their flaws were virtuous enough. There have been many more who succumbed to the illusive seduction of temporal power. When scandal and corruption came calling, their steadfast friends typically left them faster than geese flying south for the winter. Their reputation in ruins, their life experiences often followed suit. From Saul to David and his son, Solomon, to Julius Cesar to Napoleon, such rulers and kings found themselves in a downward spiral that often ended with sorrow or even death by their own or someone else's hand. Even for the ones who seemed to "get away with it," appearances could be deceiving. Broken marriages, broken children and the silent ridicule of a public who once adored them seethed behind their practiced public relations smiles. Psalms 2:2–3 speaks to their folly: "The kings of the earth take their stand and the rulers gather together against the Lord and against his Anointed One. Let us break their chains and throw off their fetters." Who needs God when success has become a habit and victory seems inevitable? While success in business or in battle may breed to some extent more success, it would serve us well to remember that failure and defeat are also part of the human drama, a part that they nor any of us can escape. Of course, defeat and failure can have its own reward. It can bring us back to a place we have forgotten. Such experiences can turn our eyes away from the kings of this world and fix our gaze on the King of Creation.

The cast of characters in this chapter are a mixed bag. Saul was the son of a big fish family in small pond. From the smallest Israelite clan, the Benjamites, he was a big, imposing specimen of a man. As impressive as he looked on the outside, he felt small on the inside. He had his doubts and said as much to Samuel. Saul could be impulsive which along with his fears and insecurities, often yielded poor results. He also had a petty and jealous side to him that fueled his darker leanings. His son, Jonathan, was different from his father. He had an air of optimism and openness that worked well with the courage that he demonstrated on more than one occasion. Then there was David. In many ways, as or more impulsive than Saul. A celebrity at a young age after disposing of Goliath, he seemed for most of his life torn between indulging his rock-star status and following God's leading. In many ways, his life was like a yo-yo, full of ups and downs. He was followed by his son, Solomon who possessed a genuine upside as a young man, but unfortunately succumbed to the downside of his father's less stellar tendencies. Finally, we have Joshua. Even though he had been mentored by Moses as his assistant, when the mantle of leadership was passed from Moses to him to lead the Israelites into the Promised Land, Joshua realized it would be a tall order indeed. He had closely observed Moses' fitful relationship with the children of Israel. He had a good idea of what he was in for. Unlike most leaders who test the political winds before acting, Joshua had a clear compass. Of course, he wasn't a king, but one who was committed to do the bidding of Yahweh, the King of Kings. Perhaps, that is in part, what saved him from falling into a life of excess and self-importance.

AN UNCERTAIN KING

The prophet and Judge, Samuel, was as tough as they came. He didn't mince his words or actions. He gave Israel an earful on more than one occasion for a variety of their missteps including their taste for foreign gods. He told them time and again the only king they needed was Yahweh. When their clamoring continued unabated, he finally relented with the warning that Yahweh would leave them to their folly.

Israel's first anointed king was Saul. A head taller than other men, strong and handsome and from a wealthy family to boot, he could have been the poster boy for what a king should look like. Like many of us, Saul depended on God until he didn't. He and his army won a string of victories on the battlefield to the applause and adoration of his people. With the wind at his back, Saul could have continued on the positive path he had forged for the nation of Israel. The trouble is that when one gets to the top of his game, the question becomes how does one stay there, especially when the voices inside his head and heart constantly remind him of his fears and insecurities? The same held true for Saul. When his army scored a spectacular victory over the Amakelites he ignored Samuel's counsel. Perhaps, he thought to himself: "Just this once, let the spoils go to the victors." Besides, his men, flushed with success, were pressuring him for the spoils along with the logic of why let healthy livestock and other valuables go to waste? So Saul did what a lot of political leaders do, he tried to have it both ways—satisfy his men and his God. The sickly livestock were sacrificed and the Amakelite king, Agag, was brought back as a prisoner. Perhaps, he might fetch a handsome ransom. What Saul had hoped was a win-win decision instead turned out to be the beginning of the end for him.

A LEADER OF EXCESS

How does one go from being a young man of legendary discernment and wisdom and the author of the Book of Proverbs to the man and king Solomon became?

Perhaps, Solomon's most famous demonstration of his prowess as a discerning leader involved the two women who both claimed to be the mother of a baby. He offered to cut the baby in two and give each woman half. The real mother was willing to give up her claim rather than have the infant killed. As a result, Solomon ordered that her baby be returned to her.

In a sense, Solomon like his father, David, before him, achieved a measure of fame and the reputation that went with it at an early age. There was little doubt that he was blessed with the gift of acute observation and discernment. He had an uncanny ability to read people and their motives. Later in life, he put the same set of skills in play that he used to settle differences like those between the two women who claimed to be the mother of the infant, to using them in business negotiations and acquiring wealth. One could say that Solomon was the original business and Wall Street entrepreneur. He knew how to work the market.

The downside of it all had to do with where and who he came from. Born from the illicit union of King David and Bathsheba, Uriah's wife, young Solomon was raised in a world of intrigue—a moving landscape of privilege and indulgence. As brave and successful as David could be on the battlefield, he proved much less effective as a father and husband. In the language of today, King David would be considered an enabler where his children were concerned as exemplified by his tragic relationship with his son, Absalom.

Not only did David often seem inadequate as a father, he appeared vulnerable to the machinations of women, especially Bathsheba. Bathsheba had David's number ever since he saw her bathing from his balcony. Solomon grew up under the careful eye of his mother's influence. Part of his observation skills were honed watching his mother bob and weave through David's chaotic court, manipulating this or that person toward her own design. Even as David drew his last breath, Bathsheba played a masterful hand in getting the tired, old king to give her son, Solomon his throne.

It didn't take long for Solomon to transition his observational savvy from mediating interpersonal conflicts to becoming a wheeler-dealer of the first order. As much money as he made, he spent even more and of course, expected the people he reigned over to pay for his lavish lifestyle. The finest food, wine, horses and whatever else caught his fancy received the green light to purchase. Solomon made sure his brand became the biggest and the best for all the world to see. The glittering lights of a desert kingdom Las Vegas would not come in even a close second.

Of course, Solomon didn't want to leave Yahweh out of the picture. He had a Temple in Jerusalem built that was the talk of the town and the region. Bronze columns, gold trim, intricate carvings, cedar and cypress were forged into a construction project that took seven years to complete.

After he had finished with the Temple, Solomon revealed his true hand—his priority. He had a palace built for himself that took thirteen years to complete. As Solomon counted his golden coins, it became in a manner of speaking, "one for God and two for Solomon."

Not only did King Solomon acquire a taste for fine food and buildings, he also developed quite a taste for fine women. He had 700 wives, including one who was the Pharaoh's daughter. Not wanting to discriminate, Solomon's harem included 300 additional Moabite, Ammonite, Edomite and other concubines. It seems as time went by, he may have preferred "the Song of Solomon" more than the "Book of Proverbs." In addition, his taste for variety in women opened the door to the foreign gods they brought with them.

Solomon did have his upside. He was an astute observer who used his skills and administrative abilities to peacefully hold his kingdom together for 40 years, no small feat for a king in that era. He made treaties with Egypt and Tyre and engaged in lucrative trade deals, seagoing and otherwise, throughout Arabia and the

Mediterranean. If only he had been a bit more frugal and less extravagant—if only he had been a better manager of the balance sheet. Many of us in today's world have our share of "if onlys." The cost of Solomon's excess was born on the backs of his people. It took a lot of money to keep the spotlights shining on his buildings and his brand. Overtaxed and forced to work on his construction projects whether they wanted to or not, the people were none too happy. Solomon took all they had and then some. Their displeasure culminated in a revolt in the northern part of the kingdom led by Jeroboam. While Solomon's army was able to put down the rebellion, it foretold of what was to come.

Solomon had a creative and determined imagination and the drive and skills to make many of his wishes come to pass. While he was perhaps, wise in his youth, "clever" might be a more accurate term to describe his adulthood. Wisdom and cleverness aren't the same. Wisdom includes humility and self-awareness while cleverness primarily requires that the ends always justify the means. As he grew older, like most of us, he became more conservative and less risk-taking. The status quo was good enough and to cover his bets, he had impressive altars built to Moabite, Ammonite and a host of other gods. It seems a clever, but not a wise decision given the promises Yahweh made and the consequences for not honoring them. For all the spectacle and glitter of Solomon's reign, it is telling that soon after he died, a revolution split his kingdom in two.

AS FOR ME AND MY HOUSE

In a way, Joshua was Moses' second chance, a chance he made the most of. We don't know much about Joshua's background except that he was the son of Nun. What we do know is that as Moses looked down from Mt. Pisgah on the land promised to his people by Yahweh, a land he would only see from a distance, he knew it was time to hand the reigns for the rest of the journey over to Joshua.

It seems worth noting that promised lands tend to already be inhabited by people who have discovered them from previous occupants. At worst, homesteaders of a land someone else feels was promised to them may see the newcomers as intruders to be resisted at all costs. Like the poster with a photograph of two Apaches standing on a bluff holding rifles that read, "Fighting illegal immigration since 1735," they like the Canaanite tribes before them, weren't about to give up the place they called home without a fight. What followed were years of warfare that in the context of that era, were as brutal and savage as modern-day wars.

Joshua's reign was one of revival—reviving the spirit and purpose of his people. At Sheehan he gathered the elders and tribal leaders together for a solemn renewal of the Covenant. He enforced a renunciation of the idolatry many Israelites had developed a taste and preference for. He challenged his people to make a choice with the words, "Choose this day whom you will serve. As for me and my house, we will serve the Lord." Their refrain was clear: "We will serve the Lord" (Joshua 24:15).

Joshua reminded his people as he does us today that we are a "covenant people" connected to each other and to our God. This is especially true in today's world where we often don't know the names of our neighbors and too often identify ourselves with political labels like liberal and conservative rather than as Christians. In the New Testament, Christian koinonia reminds us that we are part of each other in community, a community that has chosen to serve the Lord and those we come in contact with in his name. Joshua's passage also makes clear that our covenant with God promises us that he will go with us, protect and guide us, but that he expects us to respond to him in faithfulness and service.

Like most leaders who find themselves in difficult situations, it isn't hard to imagine that Joshua like Moses before him, had more than his share of doubts. It is apparent that where the Canaanites were concerned, his people were full of fear and trepidation. Israel's leader may have changed, but the people hadn't. When Joshua received his instructions that all he would need to defeat the King of Jericho was a few good men with lanterns and trumpets, he also had second thoughts about being Moses' successor. Still, after several signs of encouragement from Yahweh with knees knocking and wiping sweat from his brow, he remained obedient to the task set before him—a task that ended in a decisive victory.

For Joshua, the war he waged was not just a conflict to gain a homeland for his people. It was more than that—it was Yahweh's war, a holy war. Of course, holy wars can come in all shapes and sizes. We can see even in today's world what people are willing to do to others and themselves when they believe they are engaged in a conflict ordained by the god they believe in.

Militarily speaking, Joshua became a kind of General George Patton of his era. He was fierce and unpredictable in combatting Israel's enemies. No quarter was given. No one was spared. Jericho, Gibeon and other cities fell one by one, all burned to the ground. Men, women and children were put to the sword. As the Civil War General, William T. Sherman wrote years later, "War is hell."

It would not be until Jesus came that he and through his disciples and the Apostle, Paul, would put forth the good news that all who followed Christ were his chosen people.

LESSONS LEARNED AND OPPORTUNITIES MISSED

Saul gives us pause—that looks and status can be deceiving. Handsome, strong and from a family of means, he was an imposing figure of a man. He looked the part of a king worthy of his title and for a while, he played the part. If Saul had been a professional athlete, young boys and men would have bought and worn his jersey with pride and young women might have swooned at the sight of him.

When what others think of us begin to matter more than what God thinks of us, we can look for hard times to follow. Like Saul, we often start out relying on God, but too often when we find ourselves at the top of the ladder of this or that success, personal ambition takes over. Perhaps, we think to ourselves, "I can take it from here, God." When we move away from God's purposes, he lets us—lets us experience the consequences that are sure to follow. Our emotional and mental attitude can quickly devolve from hope and confidence to fear, anxiety, jealousy and even, paranoia.

While God sees and wants us to be the best than we can be, he gives us the freedom to do what we want to. The prophet, Samuel, grieved over Saul's wasted life. God grieves over our poor choices and the consequences that our choices reap.

Saul could have better appreciated the fine young man of virtue and courage that his son, Jonathan, had become. Even after Samuel gave him the bad news, as difficult as it would have been, he could have tried to embrace what was coming with some degree of grace. Unfortunately, deep into the dark spiral he had descended to, he was unable to make such a choice. We feel for him as we do for those we love who can't seem to come back from bad choices and circumstances. It doesn't have to be that way. A lesson worth taking from the tragedy and sorrow of Saul is that while we may move away from God, he doesn't move away from us. Each mistake is also an invitation from our Creator to accept responsibility for our poor choice and return to our father who is waiting for us.

Solomon, like the rest of us, was a mixed bag. Although he didn't come from the best of moral circumstances, the good news was that through his interpersonal, observational and business acumen, he managed to maintain the peace during his forty year reign. The bad news was although as a real estate magnate he created enough bright lights and spectacular buildings to make Las Vegas blush, the results of his efforts had more to do with appearance than with substance. What impressed his neighbors was built on the backs and through the suffering of his people.

The wisdom of Solomon was replaced by the cleverness and coldness of a man who became the king of greed and self-aggrandizement. Solomon developed an insatiable love of splendor and the ostentatious display of wealth that went with it. He moved his people from the tribal civilization of his father, David, to a relentless commercial state with extremes of wealth and poverty. With thousands of slaves and hundreds of wives, he traded the kingdom of God for a kingdom of the world. Unlike his father,

David, who confessed his errors, repented and found his way back to God, there is no evidence that Solomon did the same. Perhaps, his penchant for foreign wives and concubines and their foreign gods along with his larger than life ego, encouraged him to turn away from his Creator.

Solomon's beginning was as impressive as his end was destructive for himself and Israel. We can learn from his life that "all that glitters isn't gold" and "wisdom is to be preferred over cleverness." An essential ingredient of wisdom is humility where we rely on One who is greater than ourselves for guidance. As the scripture reminds us, "What profits a man if he gains the whole world, but loses his soul" (Matt. 16:26).

In contrast to Saul and Solomon, Joshua was a breath of fresh air. He teaches us about the importance of focus and obedience. He epitomized the message of the old hymn "Revive us Again" as he led his people back to a covenant relationship with God.

Focus and obedience also allowed Joshua to get Israel's priorities back in proper order by getting them to forsake once and for all, their worship of false idols. With a humble rather than proud heart, he demonstrated obedience and submission to God's purpose and instruction. While Saul and Solomon in different ways and for different reasons, made the mistake of putting themselves first, Joshua put God first. As a result, the nation of Israel flourished under his leadership.

Lessons we can learn from Joshua are that integrity is more important than worldly success; a humble heart bathed in prayer will help us to more clearly understand what God wants us to do; putting God first will allow us to persevere in obedience to God's purpose in our lives.

QUESTIONS FOR REFLECTION AND DISCUSSION

1. The old saying that a "man's home is his castle" points to a family's and a nation's need to feel secure and good about the place they live and call home.

    How did the people of Israel feel under the reign of Saul and Solomon about their personal security and the security of their nation?

    Can we see examples of Saul's and Solomon's errors and mistakes in our own community and nation?

2. When we are successful, we may feel like we are on top of the world or king of the hill. For many people, there is nothing that feels better than winning a contest or being number one in business.

    What are some of the dangers and risks of being on top? Does it matter how we got there?

    What are some lessons we can learn from Saul, Solomon and Joshua on how to handle success and how not to?

3. Like Saul and Solomon, do we tend to pay more attention to what other people think about us than what God thinks?

    What are some possible consequences for trying too hard to "keep up with the Joneses?"

4. Joshua was a different breed of a man. How can we benefit from the qualities he demonstrated—focus, priorities, obedience and perseverance—in today's world?

4

A Mother's Ambition

Genesis 24–27
Luke 1:46–55
Luke 2:45–50
Matthew 12:38–50
John 19:26–27

> "When Jack Burns needed to hold his mother's hand, his fingers could see in the dark."
>
> JOHN IRVING

> "A man loves his sweetheart the most, his wife the best, his mother the longest."
>
> IRISH PROVERB

> "Mothers are inscrutable beings to their sons…"
>
> A.E. COPPARD

> "All that I am or hope to be, I owe to my angel mother. I remember my mother's prayers and they have always followed me."
>
> ABRAHAM LINCOLN

WE HAVE MANY REFERENCES to mothers as well as to the idea of "Mother" in a more archetypal sense—Mother Earth, the Queen Mother, the mother lode and so on. While fathers are part of the process of conceiving a new life, it is the mother who carries and nurtures the child and from whom the child emerges nine months later. There is a special intimacy—biological and emotional—between mothers and their children. Mothers and their sons tend to have a unique sense of connection. As the quotes at the beginning of this chapter suggest, where sons are concerned, their closest relationships are often formed with their mothers. Emotional support, encouragement and an unwavering loyalty and commitment to their sons' wellbeing is a hallmark of many mothers throughout the ages. Men have been heard to say that they would rather be beaten black and blue than make their mothers cry.

Of course, mothers can also be inscrutable and manipulative on occasion as they seek to do what they think is best for their sons. Their affection can be withheld and their words can cut like sharp scissors when used as a weapon—especially with young children. In our modern age, we hear about "helicopter" parents and parents who enable their children in co-dependent relationships which don't serve the best interests of their children in the long run. That was also true in Biblical times. While no one may love a son like his mother, a mother's love can also be suffocating and smothering. When that happens, relationships with others can fracture and disintegrate, robbing a young boy of any chance of happiness outside the sphere of his mother's influence.

In Biblical times, marriages were typically arranged for a variety of economic and security-based reasons. There were not any beauty pageants or bachelor and bachelorette television competitions to watch. Of course, that isn't to suggest that a young man or woman couldn't catch the other's eye. We know that when Jacob saw Rachel he wept. On a darker note, when David saw Bathsheba bathing his pulse also quickened and unfortunately, there were no limits he would not go to in order to have her. In most parts of today's world, men and women choose who they are attracted to and whether or not they are interested in a marriage commitment. Of course, given some of the boy and girl friends our children bring home, more than one set of parents may have reconsidered the merits of the arranged marriages of old.

MOMMA'S BOY

Sometimes a person starts out life full of optimism and good intentions, but after taking a wrong turn here and there end up in a dead-end place, sad and alone. In other instances, a man or woman seems born with two strikes against him or her. Raised in the school of hard knocks, they catch a break and persevere to the point they find a good life beyond their wildest expectations. Rebekah was an interesting mix of the two life courses. The fact that her brother was Laban who proved to be a conniver par excellence suggests that her family background had a strong element of hustle and misdirection in its DNA. That said, when Abraham's servant, Eliezer, devised a test to find an appropriate wife for Isaac, the young maiden, Rebekah, passed with flying colors. Not only did she volunteer to draw water for Eliezer to drink, she went the extra mile and watered his ten thirsty camels as well. Attractive, kind and generous—Eliezer must have smiled to himself with satisfaction when he found Rebekah.

When Rebekah returned home, she showed her mother the golden ring and two bracelets Eliezer had given her. Seeing the gift of jewelry his sister had procured apparently got Laban's temperature on the uptick. He wasted no time inviting Eliezer to be their guest. Upon hearing from Eliezer what the purpose of his mission was and receiving the gifts he had brought with him, Rebekah's family agreed for her to become Isaac's bride, a decision she found favor with. However, after a night of celebration, the family hedged a bit and tried to keep Rebekah with them a while longer. Who knows why? Perhaps, they would miss her good-natured presence or perhaps, they considered the possibility that there were more gifts to be had—a skill Laban would perfect in his future dealings with Jacob. Whatever the reason, upon Eliezer's insistence and Rebekah's agreement, their caravan set out for the distant south.

Isaac saw their entourage approaching and Rebekah saw Isaac in the field. They both liked what they saw. We are told that Isaac brought Rebekah into the tent of his mother, Sarah, and took her to be his wife—and he loved her. If Rebekah and Isaac's story ended here, we could imagine them living happily ever after. But it didn't. Over time their relationship began to sour. It didn't happen overnight. Sometimes, even the sweetest love stories do not last.

As was common in those days, Rebekah was much younger than her husband. Her pregnancy with the twins, Esau and Jacob, was a difficult one. As Isaac and Rebekah grew older, they may have become distant. Esau, strong and outgoing, seems to have been the apple of his father's eye. In a sense, Jacob could not compete with his brother for his father's favor even if he had wanted to. And Rebekah wouldn't have been the first mother to dote on the child who was to some extent, left out where his father's affections were concerned. Who can say with any certainty why an estrangement occurred? What does seem clear is that in middle life Rebekah was different than the young bride who embraced her marriage and new family with enthusiasm and anticipation. Whatever the reasons, as the world closed in around her, Rebekah gave the lion's share of her attention and care to Jacob. Maybe, it was because he was second-best in his father's eyes. Esau was a man's man, a hunter—strong and assertive. If there had been football in that day, Isaac would have been in the stands cheering Esau's all-star performance. Jacob on the other hand, appeared to be more introspective, overshadowed by his larger than life older brother. Maybe Esau tried to teach Jacob how to hunt and fish and maybe Jacob tried his hand at those skills. For Esau to forgive his brother's treachery years later suggests that they did have some kind of relationship that had deeper roots. Still, the family currents pulled them apart. The high tide of Isaac reveled in the hunter's prowess and savory meals of his older son while the low evening tide of Rebekah quietly encouraged her younger son to become opportunistically adept and adaptable.

Esau's impulsiveness and lack of discernment is demonstrated when returning from a hunt, hungry and tired, he traded

A MOTHER'S AMBITION

his birthright to Jacob for a bowl of stew. It could have been that Esau didn't think his brother, Jacob, would hold him to the agreement. Perhaps, like the ensuing deception planned by Rebekah and carried out by Jacob, his trade of stew for a birthright was the first act in Rebekah's play for her younger son to inherit what was due Esau. Whatever the reason, it worked. Clothed in his brother's finest, covered with goat skins, and bearing a bowl of stew, Jacob deceived his nearly blind father, Isaac who unknowingly bestowed his older brother's birthright upon him.

Like many deceptions born of ambition, Rebekah and Jacob's well-executed plan had unintended consequences. Two are of particular note. First, Jacob may have stolen his brother's birthright, but in the process, he also broke his father's heart. In addition, while Isaac couldn't restore the birthright to his older son, Esau would still be his favorite and Jacob had essentially diminished what was left of his relationship with his father. Second, while probably anticipated to some degree, Esau's rage ran unabated and put Jacob's life in peril. The long and short of it was that if Esau got hold of Jacob, a birthright would be of no use to a dead man.

The situation was getting messy. Rebekah needed a new plan to cover the old one if Jacob was to survive. Keeping her wits about her, she persuaded Isaac that it would be best for Jacob to go to her brother Laban for a cooling off period and to find a proper wife. In discussing the situation with her son, she most likely was more to the point—that Jacob should run for his life!

A MOTHER UNEXPECTED

What on earth would you think if God's messenger, Gabriel, suddenly appeared and told you that you would be the vessel through which the promised one, the Messiah, would come into the world? It was hard enough for a young woman living in a dusty backwater excuse of a town called Nazareth to find a decent husband—and Mary had accomplished that. Joseph was a carpenter and by all accounts, a good and decent man. Besides, she was already spoken for, betrothed to Joseph. And then Gabriel informs her that she was indeed, already spoken for, but not by Joseph—by God himself. What was a young woman from Nazareth who was hardly old enough to have a child to think?

How did Mary's revelation happen—that she would be mother to the Savior of the world? Perhaps, it began in her dreams in fits and whispers, in ways that both transfixed her expectation of the honor of it all along with the unease of dark shadows of doubt hiding in the woods. And when God breathed himself into her—when her body began to change and she could feel life moving inside her—how could this be? Even after she had embraced her call with humility and submission to God's will along with the support of Joseph, she still must have rubbed her growing belly and mumbled to herself—how can this be? Yet, it was to be and has been "being" ever since. Mary who was little more than a girl, embraced the role she was to play with grace and humility. The young maiden who accepted both the blessing of bearing and being mother to the Christ child would also come to embody the sorrow of what was to come.

First, came the birth of the baby Jesus in Bethlehem. A long and tiring journey for Mary and Joseph to register for the Roman Census found them looking for a place to stay. All the accommodations were taken, even at the low-rent inns. They ended up in a manger where she gave birth to the Messiah—not in a palace of gold and opulence, but in a palace of straw and wood. No dignitaries of the king's court were there to witness and honor the Savior's birth, only Mary and Joseph and perhaps, a braying donkey or two. The shepherds came as did the three wise men. What they reported was nothing short of astounding—angels singing in a heavenly chorus, a luminous north star, frankincense and myrrh—foretold that their child would be shepherd to the least of those and king of all. Still, we are reminded in the face of all the amazing events as well as the frustrations that accompanied them, Mary's patience and forbearing remained. While others marveled at the miracle of it all, she "kept all these things and pondered them in her heart" (Luke 2:19).

A Mother's Ambition

We can imagine the childhood of young Jesus, one of several brothers and sisters. He was a part of them, but at the same time apart from them—set aside for something they may have sensed at times, but could have no way of understanding what it might be. No doubt, he played with his siblings, skinned his knees and acted like other young boys in his village. Perhaps, on other occasions Mary may have found him sitting on a rock looking at some distant place only he could see. Like others in the village, he learned the craft of his father, Joseph, who was a carpenter by trade.

For most of Jesus' growing up years, we are told very little. Scriptures tell us that when he was brought to the Temple as was the custom, Old Simeon, a faithful prophet of God, took the baby Jesus in his arms and blessed God, thanking him for the fulfillment of the promise that he would live to see the Christ child. We are told that Mary and Joseph marveled at what Simeon said about their son. When Simeon told Mary that "a sword would pierce through her soul also" (Luke 2:35), she carried that dark prediction in silence.

We also find a twelve year-old Jesus separated from his parents in the hustle and bustle of their pilgrimage to Jerusalem for the Feast of the Passover. In this event, we find Mary rebuking her son as any mother would for the worry and anxiety he had caused her and his father. Looking for a lost child for three days is no laughing matter. We can imagine the panic that must have over-taken Mary as she and Joseph searched the streets and byways for their son. What is unusual in this narrative is Jesus' response. When Jesus, sitting in the midst of teachers astonished by his insights and wisdom, replied to his Mother, he responded in a way that demonstrated his independence and the purpose that he was being prepared for. Mary may have been taken aback and even a bit confused when her twelve year-old son shrugged and said, "Why do you seek me? Don't you know that I must be about my father's business" (Luke 2:49)? Can we imagine a response like that from one of our children we had been searching high and low for three days straight? Although Mary had accepted and even embraced her duty as being the mother of the long-awaited

Messiah, it must have been to some degree, a schizoid experience. On the one hand, she loved him as her earthly son even though in her heart of hearts she knew he was much more than that. On the other hand, much of what her son was about was beyond her ability to understand. Mary was caught between two worlds, alternating between the normal joys and stresses of motherhood and at the same time, feeling as she were operating in a fog where her son, Jesus was concerned.

The first public miracle of Jesus occurred at a wedding feast in Cana. Apparently, Mary was the one on the hostess committee in charge of the wine. When they ran out, she went to her eldest son with the simple statement, "they ran out of wine." Mary's request suggests the possibility that she was already aware of the gifts of her first-born. Although he complied with his mother's request, Jesus' reply was at best, a reprimand of sorts when he said, "Woman, what does your concern have to do with me? My hour has not yet come" (John 2:4). We notice that on this occasion as with his other recorded interaction with his mother, Jesus refers to her as woman rather than mother.

As Jesus began his public ministry with his disciples, the distance between him and his Mother and the rest of his family grew. Mary like all mothers who have sons, didn't understand her eldest, but even more so why her son needed to wander all over the place, preaching to friend and foe alike? Why couldn't he be a Messiah "and" a carpenter in Nazareth? Wishful thinking, yes, but then as now, a mother's heart wants what it wants.

At first, things went well enough. Large crowds were fed and moved by his words and actions—and disciples joined in his cause. The scent of trouble also began to follow him as the Pharisees plotted with Herod's crew to do him in. They had already beheaded John the Baptist. Could he be next? Over time his situation seemed to be getting worse and rather tamping things down a bit, Mary's son only added fuel to the fire. When the scribes came down from Jerusalem and accused him of being the spawn of Satan, instead of retreating, Jesus gave them a healthy dose of hell.

Folks were talking. The gossip was moving like an out-of-control brush fire. Thank goodness, they didn't have the internet in those days. People who had known Jesus from when he was a child scratched their heads and whispered that he must be out of his mind. Gathered in groups around Nazareth, in today's parlance, they might have said things like, "The boy needs professional help;" "He needs to go see that Psychiatrist, Dr. Simon;" or "He needs to be locked up for his own good before he gives our town an even worse reputation than it already has."

After a family meeting, Mary and his brothers planned to do an intervention with Jesus. They called to him from outside a group of people he was meeting with. When informed that his mother and brothers wanted to talk to him, he did not go to them, but instead replied, "Who is my mother, or my brothers?" Looking at the people who sat before him, he continued: "here are my mother and brothers! For whoever does the will of God is my brother and my sister and my mother" (Matt. 12:49–50). It may have been at that moment that the sword that Simeon had predicted years earlier, pierced a mother's soul.

From the time he was twelve years old, nowhere in the Gospels do we find Jesus expressing anything approaching the sentimental exchanges that are often found between a mother and her son. In a sense, it must have been frustrating for both of them. Mary, his earthly mother did not understand the big picture of his mission and worried about the coming storm of torment her mother's intuition signaled deep within her. Jesus, knowing time was short, seemed to have less and less time for his mother and family. She didn't understand. There was no way she could. The Good News he offered was bad news to many who were loyal to the religious and political establishment. Then came that terrible day at Calvary.

Mary stood near her son's cross, helpless and heartbroken. Next to her stood Jesus' disciple, John. Her mother's instincts were of no use now. What thoughts and feelings must have raced through her mind and heart? Where were the angels? Why had they not delivered him? What about his own powers that healed the afflicted and even brought back Lazarus from the dead? Why could he not save himself? And then it happened. In one of Jesus' final acts of compassion, he looked down at his mother. Nailed to a cross, broken and bleeding, he looked down from his crown of thorns and spoke to her: "Behold your son," he said through bruised and cracked lips. Shifting his gaze to his beloved disciple, he said, "Behold your mother" (John 19:26–27). Mother and son, their eyes meeting one last time, crossed a gulf that had separated them from the temporal to the eternal. In the end, Jesus gave her a flesh and blood son to love and be loved by. He gave her a relationship with his "beloved" disciple and as far as this world goes, the best part of himself that he could offer.

The last time we see Mary is in the upper room with the disciples on the Day of Pentecost when the Spirit was poured out upon them. The last picture we have of Mary is as a Spirit-filled Christ follower worshipping in community.

LESSONS LEARNED AND OPPORTUNITIES MISSED

Given the historical context of her time and the general plight of women in that era, we should not be too hard on Rebekah. What she did has been repeated time and again throughout the ages. A mother's ambition or father's for that matter, can blind itself to the consequences of choices made. When Jacob became uneasy about his mother's plan, Rebekah told her son that the curse would be on her rather than on him and indeed, it was. It is also ironic that her brother, Laban, deceived Jacob much in the same manner that Jacob deceived Esau and his father, Isaac. It seems that what goes around, does indeed, come around.

Deception and betrayal may yield short-term rewards, but at the expense of life-long sorrow and suffering. The good news from his mother's point of view was that her son, Jacob, did receive Isaac's blessing and Esau's birth-right. The bad news was that she would never see her son again. Her estranged relationship with her husband most likely became even more estranged. And Esau would have nothing to do with her for the rest of her life. While we don't know the exact circumstances of Rebekah's death, it appears that she died alone and was buried in a cave at Machpelah.

Taking a larger and longer view, we can see that even with the opportunities that Rebekah missed and the ones she should not have taken advantage of, God still does his work. Esau forgave his brother and they wept with joy and relief at their meeting after so many years of being apart. Maybe time does heal all wounds. We are fortunate that God's grace often trumps his sense of justice. A conniving crook named Jacob became the father of the twelve tribes of Israel. Who would have ever thought that such a thing would be part of God's grand plan?

With Mary it is somewhat of a different story. While both Rebekah and Mary demonstrated humility and kindness as young woman, Mary's path was more complicated and at times, confusing. Rebekah's ambition was to procure a birth-right for her son, Jacob, that wasn't his. Mary's ambition was to the best of her ability, help her son, Jesus, fulfill his birth-right, one that would save the world from itself.

There are portraits of Mary where she is described and depicted in many different ways. What is clear from what we know of her is that she was humble and obedient to a task that bordered on the impossible for any human being. She had a devotion to and love of God in which she demonstrated faithfulness, poise and perseverance. At its best, a mother's love is much like God's love. It is a love that is unceasing, one that walks both ahead and behind the beloved—ahead clearing the loved one's path and preparing the way and behind, picking up the broken pieces of damaged lives in an effort to make them whole again.

QUESTIONS FOR REFLECTION AND DISCUSSION

1. What are some ways ambition can be used for good? Can you think of any Biblical examples? What about personal ones? What are some ways ambition can become destructive?

2. Compare women in Biblical times to women today. What advantages do women have today that they didn't have in the time that Mary lived? Are there any downsides to being a modern woman?

3. Deception, especially self-deception, may be the greatest challenge to being a follower of Christ. Like Rebekah, we can often convince ourselves and justify choices that are destructive to ourselves and those we hold most dear. Rebekah got what she wanted through deception and betrayal and a whole lot more that she didn't want. Was it worth it?

4. All mothers have issues with their sons and other children. What issues do modern mothers share with Mary? What qualities did Mary possess and demonstrate in her life that could help us to become better mothers and fathers?

5

A Good Marriage Is Hard to Find

Genesis 29–31
Ruth 1–4
Mark 10:7–9

> "You know you're in love when you can't fall asleep
> because reality is really better than your dreams."
> DR. SEUSS

> "Success in marriage is more than finding the right person;
> it is a matter of being the right person."
> RABBI B.R. BRICKNER

> "Being deeply loved by someone gives you strength,
> while loving someone deeply gives you courage."
> LAO TZU

> "Marriage is our last, best chance to grow up."
> JOSEPH BARTH

WHAT DOES IT MEAN to be married? When we look at what is going on in our world today we can see that it means different things to different people. For better or worse, different cultural influences also influence our perceptions of marriage. Women no longer are expected to suffer physical and emotional abuse in silence and men have become increasingly aware that marriage is also a partnership where both husband and wife need to cultivate a servant's heart.

Tensions often arise as new thinking and preferences challenge more traditional views of marriage and family. Change often seems to be the only constant. Some even make the claim that traditional marriage is nothing more than an archaic relic of the past. And then there is the mix of blended families where couples who marry bring with them children and issues from their previous marriage. While the second-time-around may be the charm in one sense, it also brings with it, a dynamic and sometimes frustrating history. When past meets present in such situations, adjustments and an extra dose of compassion, patience and forgiveness are often required.

Growing pains are part of the marriage process in even the best of relationships. Marriage comprises a kind of unique trinity. There is the personality and experiences of the husband as well as the wife. There is also the marriage, the union of husband and wife where two are becoming one. While a physical union may be a relatively straightforward and pleasurable experience, emotional connections often take time. The union is the most vulnerable part of the marriage trinity. "You don't cook like my mother" or "Why can't you be understanding like my father" have been a point of conflict in more than one early marriage conversation. Becoming one will sometimes go smoothly—even joyously. On other occasions, it may find itself bruised and even broken in one of life's many ditches. Like an infant child, the infant marriage requires that it be handled with care so that it can grow healthy and mature deeply. For marriage to work, we have to learn to put the other first. The same holds true when we have a child. If as parents, we don't put our child first, when he or she grows up, they will put what we have tried to teach them us last. The question also arises: how does a parent nurture his or her spouse while fully attending to one's child? It's easier said than done.

AS THE HEART TURNS

In Biblical times, women had virtually no rights and were dependent on their father and family. They were to be seen and not heard. When Jacob saw Rachel, he watered her father's flock, kissed her and wept—in that order. Apparently her beauty overwhelmed him and he cried tears of joy. Of course, as it turns out, his weeping was only the beginning of the tears he would cry. While for the rest of his life, Jacob would never get over the beauty of his beloved Rachel, from that time forward he would have ample opportunity to express tears of frustration and disappointment as he dealt with Rachel and her family.

After Jacob had worked seven years for the hand of Rachel, Laban tricked him into marrying her older sister, Leah, instead. Maybe it was too much wine or too much dancing. Whatever the case, Jacob spent his wedding night with Leah. Much to his chagrin, he realized Laban's deception the next morning. Of course, the wily Laban had an angle and wrestled another seven year commitment from Jacob in order to procure the hand of Rachel.

When Jacob was finally able to marry Rachel, one can imagine his joy—that the good times were just beginning. Jacob was mistaken. Instead of wedded bliss, he had just punched his ticket for a merry-go-round of bitterness, petulance and deception. It seems as he had transitioned from being the son of a strong-willed mother to the husband of a strong-willed wife. There was also the situation of his wives—two sisters, one more beautiful than the other. Leah, the weak-eyed older sister, was good-hearted enough, but not so good-looking—at least, not to Jacob. To a careful eye, marrying two sisters should in and of itself have been viewed as fraught with danger. Let the good times begin, indeed!

Blended families of today along with the various rivalries among children and adults have nothing on the issues surrounding the pressure of marriage and parenting during Biblical times. Multiple wives, concubines and family intrigue were dicey enough to make modern soap operas blush. Perhaps, it shouldn't have surprised Jacob although it probably did. Marrying the daughters of his mother's brother, Uncle Laban—the same mother who schooled him in the art of deception that allowed him to steal his brother, Esau's birthright—didn't bode well for a clear and honest marriage arrangement. The fact that Laban told Jacob that he would rather give Rachel to Jacob than to another man also demonstrates that Rachel had little say in the matter. Still, it seems clear enough that Rachel did respond to Jacob's adoration and affection.

BEAUTY IS AS BEAUTY DOES

What about Rachel? She was beautiful and the apple of Jacob's eye. We aren't provided much more detail about Rachel other than she was beautiful. If we read the scripture for what it says, one could conclude that there was little to recommend Rachel other than her beauty. Perhaps, there was more to her story. Perhaps, she felt undone by her father's shenanigans involving her sister and Jacob. She may have genuinely cared for Jacob, especially given his commitment to work seven additional years in order to marry her. Yet, given her protracted inclination toward envy and bitterness and quarreling with her sister, Leah, she does not come across as a very mature or sympathetic character.

Sibling rivalry then and now is nothing new. Cain and Abel, Jacob and Esau and Joseph and his brothers all demonstrate how important parental relationships are in providing a nurturing family environment. Still, even with the influence of family dynamics and environment and her apparent beauty, Rachel could have made different choices. As difficult as it might have been, she could have reached out to Leah and tried to make room for her in the life and affection of Jacob and herself. But she didn't. Stress and frustration for Jacob, loneliness and despair for her sister, Leah, and unhappiness for Rachel herself ended up being the unfortunate fruit that her circumstances, attitude and choices bore.

WHERE YOU GO

Hunger and famine are strong motivators, strong enough for an Israelite husband and wife with two sons to immigrate to Moab. The wife was Naomi and after her husband died, her two sons ended up marrying Moabite women. Unfortunately, Naomi's sons also died. All that remained was her and her two daughters-in-law, Ruth and Orpah. Unlike Laban and his daughters, Naomi, Orpah and Ruth loved and supported each other. Deciding to return to her hometown in Judah, Naomi implored her two daughters-in-law to return to their families and find themselves another husband. When she insisted that they turn back and not follow her, they wept with grief. Orpah kissed her mother-in-law and did as Naomi instructed, but Ruth "clung" to Naomi and said, " . . . wherever you go, I will go . . . your people shall be my people. And your God, my God" (Ruth 1:16). When Naomi realized that Ruth was just as determined to go with her as she was for Ruth to return to her family, she relented.

What Naomi told Ruth and Orpah to do, she did out of love. She didn't want to be a burden to them and knew their chances at finding another husband were better without her being around. Ruth refused Naomi's request out of love as well. She would not abandon her beloved Mother-in-law. They would cast their lots in the future together. After Naomi fussed a bit with Ruth about staying with her and finally accepting Ruth's determined decision with a sigh, one can imagine Naomi walking toward Bethlehem with the hint of a smile on her face.

Apparently Naomi and her husband were held in high regard because it seems that most of Bethlehem put out the "welcome home" banner when Naomi and Ruth arrived. Being from Moab gave Ruth a hint of the exotic. She also was a different kind of woman—not only attractive, but possessing a kind of determined spunk that attracted some men and probably intimidated others. One man who took special notice was Boaz, a man of great wealth. He may have been a little long in the tooth, but his eyesight was good enough to notice a pretty Moabitess gathering grain left by his reapers. Boaz wasn't a man to waste time. He gave Ruth a VIP pass to his fields that included all the grain she needed, cool water when she was thirsty, food when she was hungry and his personal guarantee of protection and safety. Others might look down on her or try to take advantage of her because she was a foreigner, but not Boaz, a man of character and kindness. To him, Ruth was both pleasing to his eye and to his heart.

Naomi was both shrewd and tough. She was determined to fix Ruth up with a good husband and what better time to do it than harvest time? She saw the writing on the wall—Boaz might be a careful man, but he was a smitten careful man. Following Naomi's instructions to the letter, Ruth won Boaz's heart and became his wife. An uncertain journey she chose to go on with Naomi had reached a contented conclusion.

LESSONS LEARNED AND OPPORTUNITIES MISSED

Three women—two of them, Rachel and Ruth, both graced with beauty—had to respond to challenging circumstances in their lives that they had no control over. Rachel came from a family with a tradition of deception whose father exemplified a modern-day con artist and opportunist. Then there was her less desirable sister, Leah, who stayed in the background, yearning for the attention her sister took for granted. While we don't know the family history of Ruth's parents and siblings, the love and loyalty she had for Naomi speaks volumes about her strength of character and personal determination.

There was a time when Israelites would choose an animal to be the symbolic scapegoat to take on all the sins of the people. At the conclusion of the ceremony, they would drive the hapless animal out into the wilderness to die. In many contemporary families, one member for a variety of reasons, often becomes the family scapegoat. Although it is typically one of the children, it can on occasion, also be one of the parents. Whoever it turns out to be, he or she tends to be the family member who is most emotionally and often physically dependent on the family system. The family scapegoat may be identified as the one who always seems to get it wrong, making one mistake after another he or she may be considered too fragile to meet expectations that other members of the family are expected to meet. Often, the scapegoat may also be blamed for a given family's general unhappiness or misfortune. Even in extreme cases of physical abuse, one child is often abused in ways his or her other siblings are not.

Leah wasn't the pretty daughter. In a sense, she seemed to be something of a scapegoat. She knew what it felt like to always be second best. While Leah may have been attractive enough, her prospects for marriage were apparently as poor as her eyesight. Leah may have loved Jacob, but Jacob loved Rachel. Of course, that didn't keep Jacob from sleeping with her. Although she kept hoping that bearing sons for Jacob that Rachel could not would result with him in the end, loving her. It didn't happen. Love often distorts our perceptions. Jacob did not have the "eyes to see" Leah's love and in Rachel, for whatever reason, he saw what he wanted to see. And then there was also Leah's distorted perception—she continued to hope against hope that if she gave Jacob enough children, he would come to love her as much as she loved him. For Leah, like many family scapegoats, "down and out" often becomes the norm. An interesting irony is that since family scapegoats know what it feels like to be blamed and picked on, they can also become the most compassionate and understanding member of a given family. Despondent and feeling abandoned, Leah still had enough faith to turn to God in her time of need and he came to her as he does to each of us—not at the end of our suffering, but in the middle of it. God came to Leah and promised her a blessing that he delivered on—that along with her sister, Rachel, She would be mother to the twelve tribes of Israel.

The irony of Rachel's missed opportunities is that in spite of her jealousy, complaints and frequent displays of temper, God blessed her with a husband who loved her to his last breath and from her sons and her sister Leah's, the twelve tribes of Israel emerged. The downside of it all was the strife and discontent that seemed to constantly seep into her life and the lives of those around her. From the theft of a birthright to a conniving, dishonest father to the pressure of being primarily a tribal beauty queen, may have stacked the deck against Rachel. Still, she could have at least tried to reshuffle it and play a different hand.

While Rachel and to some extent, Leah, offer us a lesson to be learned from missed opportunities, we find that Ruth was cut from a different cloth.

Mother-in-law jokes are the common fare of comedians as are in-laws in general. Since the beginning of time, some mothers are convinced that no woman is good enough for their sons. And of course, they can communicate that notion to their daughters-in-law in a variety of unpleasant ways. That is what makes the story of Ruth and Naomi all the more remarkable. Ruth held a deep respect and love for her mother-in-law. In fact, Ruth's name means friend or refreshment, a name she represented well. Ruth was determined to stick with Naomi through thick and thin, regardless of the cost.

All of us have a "shadow side," the part of ourselves that we would prefer the world not see—the part that is vulnerable to fear, insecurity and prejudice. We also have another side that represents our "best selves," the side that enlarges our capacity to love and be kind. Ruth's loyalty to her mother-in-law, her bold spirit and her capacity to love enabled her to listen to Naomi's guidance and make the best of her second chance.

An interesting point is that in the eyes of the world, Ruth should have followed her sister-in-law, Orpah, back to her family of origin among her own people. The wisdom of the world would espouse that Ruth's odds for finding another husband would be better if she cut her losses with Naomi and played the odds. Ruth chose instead, the wisdom of the spirit and what to many must have seemed a poor choice, turned out to be the right one. Boaz saw the same qualities in Ruth that Naomi knew all too well. Like tends to attract like. Ruth's loyalty to Naomi was extended to Boaz and of course, loyalty is also related to trust. If we are loyal to someone, we inevitably trust them.

The Apostle Paul's great hymn of love in 1st Corinthians, chapter thirteen, defines the dimensions of love that Ruth embodied:

- Love is patient;
- Love is kind;
- Love is not envious or boastful;
- It does not insist on its own way;
- It is not irritable or resentful;
- It does not rejoice in wrongdoing, but rejoices in the right;
- It bears all things, believes all things, hopes all things, endures all things . . .
- And now faith, hope and love abide, these three, and the greatest of these is love.

When Ruth and Boaz had a son, they named him Obed. Naomi came and took care of him and lived with them for the rest of her days. Obed had a son named Jesse, the father of David. No one could have predicted that a down-on-her-luck young woman from Moab who made her way with her mother-in-law to Bethlehem would bear a son whose lineage would result in the greatest king Israel would ever have—a lineage that would be connected to the long-awaited Messiah.

In marriage, someone else cannot make up for what is missing in us. We each have to do our own homework in life and in relationships. Becoming one in a marriage is an ongoing process that require us to put someone else's needs before our own. A loving and loyal person makes a loving and loyal husband or wife. Even in the most loving of marriages, more than enough challenges and difficulties are also part of the story. That said, Paul's hymn and the example of Jesus shows us how to become our "best selves" in a marriage relationship. Rachel, Leah and Jacob had Rebekkah and Laban as their role models while Ruth had Naomi. Still, they had as we do, choices to make and consequences to bear.

QUESTIONS FOR REFLECTION AND DISCUSSION

1. How do family environments and experiences influence our personalities, attitudes and the adults we come to be?
2. What are some differences between Jacob's, Rachel's and Leah's family and Ruth and her mother-in-law, Naomi?
3. Even if we come from difficult family circumstances, do we still to some extent, choose who we become? Are we still responsible for the choices we make? Rachel, Leah, Ruth and Naomi all faced difficult challenges. How did the way each of them responded to their respective dilemma affect their outcomes?
4. What role did their faith play in their choices? What role does it play in our decision-making?
5. In what ways do Paul's hymn of love in Corinthians and Jesus' example demonstrate the qualities of a good marriage?

6

When Beauty Is Only Skin Deep
Judges 16
The Book of Esther

> "Beauty may have fair leaves, yet bitter fruit."
> ENGLISH PROVERB

> "Lust is the craving for salt of a man who is dying of thirst."
> FREDERICK BUECHNER

> "We are not punished for our sins, but by them."
> ELBERT HUBBARD

THERE IS A REASON why big-time beauty pageants typically focus on the swim-suit competition while paying lip service to the assessment of the contestants' intellectual abilities. Ratings. Such events are more about outward appearance than inner beauty. Of course, the two are not mutually exclusive, but a thousand lustful eyes don't tune in to hear how Miss Universe plans to be an advocate for world peace. The same can be said for actors, rock stars, athletes, and fashion models. How to look young and perform while becoming older—a challenge that the cosmetic industry has embraced with spectacular profits from men and women alike. Modern folks want to look their best as they check themselves against their peers as well as in the hallway mirror.

It is important to note that cosmetic surgery has its virtues. Children with cleft palates, burn victims and even drooping eyelids have improved the quality of countless lives that would otherwise be lost to needless suffering. And there is nothing wrong with coloring one's hair, whitening one's teeth, or working out to get into better shape, especially when it's more about one's health than one's vanity. Unfortunately, dyed hair, trampoline skin, and artificial suntans don't stop the aging process and has little to do with one's inner beauty and intrinsic worth.

Along with outward appearances, strength, agility and financial wealth—physical and economic power—are given a high priority in our contemporary world. It doesn't require much discernment to understand why a beautiful young woman finds an eighty year old man attractive. It's not his jet-black hair, suntan, white teeth or work-out routine. It's his bank account. Handsome sports celebrities blessed with great physical strength and athletic skills are not typically swooned over because of their moral character. Humility, a servant's heart, and self-respect don't sell NFL jerseys. Winning championships, pageants of one sort or another and being number one sells jerseys, boosts ratings, and increases profits.

Pride is no longer one of the seven deadly sins. It has become a virtue as has deception, deceit, and manipulation as evidenced by such successful television shows as "Survivor." Most anything goes these days as long as one wins. Where victories and trophies are concerned, the ends justify the means. In many ways, not much has changed since Samson and Delilah and Susanna and Queen Vashti lived.

THE STRONGEST MAN IN THE WORLD

Samson was something to behold! If he had lived in today's world, he would have been the Super Bowl MVP, winner of Olympic gold, most eligible bachelor and so on. Unlike many heroes who become legends long after they have passed away, Samson lived his legend in high definition and full color in the here and now. Although in some ways, the life he lived seems an ill fit for him being the last of Israel's Judges. We think of an ideal judge as being clear-eyed, self-disciplined, and diplomatic with a laser-like focus on what was best for his or her people in keeping God's commandments. Samson, instead, was impulsive, self-indulgent and a practical joker and gambler with something of a mean streak when he lost. He also had a taste for all kinds of women, especially those of the Philistine tribe.

Samson was raised to be a Nazrite, one who adhered to a number of requirements, including abstaining from wine and spirits and not shaving his beard or cutting his hair. Things went well enough until he came of age and fell for a Philistine woman who he decided to marry over the objections of his parents and contrary to his Nazrite vows. And yet, in spite of Samson's rebellious spirit and impulsive nature, God blessed him with incredible strength.

While on his way to marry Timnah, his Philistine wife-to-be, he quickly dispatched a lion who attacked him, ripping the animal from stem to stern. Keeping it secret, we see the practical joker side of Samson when he gave his thirty Philistine groomsmen a riddle and made a bet that they couldn't answer. Unfortunately, they weren't in a joking mood and after threatening to burn Timnah and her family alive, she revealed the answer to the riddle. In short order, Samson went from practical joker to sore loser. Although perhaps not apparent to him, from that point on, the road for Samson began to point downhill.

A hair-trigger temper, a self-indulgent spirit, a big ego and superhuman strength taken together don't foretell much chance of a happy ending. Samson found killing Philistines as easy as killing lions. When he found that his bride-to-be had been given in marriage by her father to one of the groomsmen, Samson made sure that the Philistine crops were burned. When the Philistines found out what happened and who was responsible they retaliated not directly against Samson, but instead, burned Timnah and her father to death. Poor Timnah, she went from being a starry-eyed victim of love to a wide-eyed victim of terror her famous suitor had put in motion.

Enraged, Samson seemed to focus as much or more on the wrong that had been done to him and his reputation. After slaughtering more Philistines, he said, "I have done to them what they did to me." Maybe he did miss Timnah to some extent, but it was she and her father who were burned alive, not Samson. Given his pride and temperamental nature, personal affronts played easily into his quick temper.

Possessing superhuman strength and cleverness, Samson proved to be a particularly sensitive thorn in the Philistines' backside. This is nowhere more apparent than when he once again tricked the Philistines and killed one thousand of them not with a magical sword, but with nothing more than the jawbone of an ass.

SAID THE SPIDER TO THE FLY

To Samson, his life, more or less, seemed good enough. Killing Philistines and pursuing women appeared to be where his primary talents lay and he made full use of them. And then, along came Delilah. Was it her beauty or her skills of seduction? We don't know for certain, but whatever it was, she had Samson's number. We are told that Samson fell in love with her. We are also told that the Philistines offered her a large sum of silver to find out the secret to Samson's strength.

Once again, we see the practical joker side of Samson as he teases his beloved, Delilah, time and again when she asks him to reveal his closely guarded secret. Maybe it was Delilah's cajoling or maybe the game got old and Samson was tired of playing it. Or maybe, it was more like the times we feel we are at our most clever and events transpire that remind us that we aren't as smart as we thought we were. Whatever the reason, he finally told her—it was the hair. The long, flowing locks he combed and fussed over were the key to his strength. With the nagging finally put to rest and a skin of good wine in his belly, Samson settled into a good night's sleep. When he awoke, his countenance had changed. The manicured mane of a champion had been replaced by the crew-cut of a prison inmate. After his eyes were gouged out by the Philistines, they ridiculed and made sport of him. Like Sisyphus rolling a stone up a mountain for eternity, Samson turned the stone grinding wheel of the mill day after day. The tormenter had finally become the tormented.

We don't know what happened to Delilah after Samson was carted off in chains. It is easy enough to look at her with the jaundiced eye of a Judas. As is usually the case, there was probably more to the story of Samson and Delilah's relationship than meets the eye. There seems to be at least some evidence that Delilah put off the Philistines for a time. At some point, they ran out of patience, became more intimidating, and made her an offer she couldn't refuse. Delilah only had to recall what they had done to Timnah and her father to realize that a bag of silver coins might be a better choice for her than being burned alive.

She and Samson had their moments. Being on the arm of a living legend had its rewards—and challenges as well. And Delilah knew Samson was no dummy. They played their game, her asking for his secret and him teasing her and making fools of the Philistines. Samson knew the Philistines were always plotting against him. Perhaps, she saw his eyebrows arch in a teasing kind of suspicion when she questioned him and he tricked her. The questions remain: Why did Delilah betray Samson and even more-so, why did Samson let her?

UNINTENDED CONSEQUENCES

We can imagine the celebration that ensued with the capture of Samson. The Philistines must have been giddy with excitement. The bain of their existence had finally been brought low. Put on the party hats, pour the champagne and strike up the marching band. Let the games begin. Make the blind man dance and sing and bump into things.

The trouble with such events is that the first taste of torment for those seeking revenge is always the sweetest. As time passes, the taste for it doesn't last as long in one's mouth. Trotting Samson out to perform for them began to grow a bit stale over time. Blind and ill-kept, he was but a shadow of the invincible conqueror he once was. Still, it was tradition to parade him out for a dose of ridicule whenever they made sacrifices to their god, Dagon. What the Philistines didn't know, perhaps because they had not been paying attention, was that Samson's hair, salt and pepper gray by now, had been growing longer. He had repented and asked God for one last redemptive favor—that his strength would return to him for one last time. So as the besotted Philistines jeered and hooted and tossed pieces of half-eaten fruit at the blind, scarred shell of a man, he pulled the temple down on their heads. One can't help but wonder if Samson the old trickster, raised his face to the hills with a look of satisfaction as he brought the pillars down with the last ounce of his strength.

WHEN BEAUTY RUNS DEEP

Beautiful women have been pursued by men throughout history. From Bathsheba to Helen of Troy, lives have been sacrificed and wars fought to win this or that Prince's or King's object of desire and affection. Of course, looking only at a woman's physical attributes rather than what is on the inside ends up objectifying her and leaves the would-be suitor with either "fool's gold" as in "looks can be deceiving" or even worse, missing the mark of all that she is and can be.

From ancient texts emerges the story of Susanna, a beautiful, young Hebrew wife who two lecherous old men tried to blackmail in an effort to get her to succumb to their sexual desires. After spying on her, they ended up concocting a plan. After she dismissed her maids and was bathing in her garden pool, the two emerged from where they had been hiding. Their demands were to the point. Either Susanna would satisfy their sexual lust or they would accuse her of adultery with a young lover. If she refused they would testify against her. The punishment for such an offense was death by stoning. Given that they were also judges and acquaintances of her husband, the two predatory lechers were confident their lustful dreams were about to be fulfilled. Susanna faced a difficult choice—death or dishonor.

She refused their offer. The result of the following day's proceedings was that the two elderly Judges testimony was accepted despite Susanna's proclamations of innocence. As she was led away to be stoned, she prayed to God for deliverance. In answer to her prayer, he sent a young man—a lawyer named Daniel—who insisted on questioning the two elders separately to be sure an innocent person wasn't being put to death. Daniel asked the two men under which kind of tree did Susanna meet her lover. One said a mastick, a smaller tree while the other claimed the two lovers met under a holm which was much larger. Their lie was apparent and they were thrown off a cliff as a result—not exactly what they originally had in mind.

There is also the story of another beautiful young woman who was observed bathing on her rooftop. Bathsheba was not approached by two old lustful lechers. She was instead, enticed by a lustful king who was willing to go to any lengths to have her. And get her he did. As beautiful as she may have been, she was no Susanna. Caught naked in a garden pool by two prominent and powerful old men who wanted her body, Susanna decided her honor and self-respect were more important to her—even if the cost was her life.

Finally, in the book of Esther, there is a poignant example of another woman who like Susanna, saw herself as more than a trophy wife to the king. Queen Vashti, wife of Xerxes was known far and wide for her spectacular beauty. The King of Persia was well-known for parties and celebrations. No one did it better. No expense was spared. All the in-crowd and the beautiful people—the shakers and movers—attended. The wine was free-flowing and tables were adorned with exotic foods from faraway places. The entertainment was non-stop from musicians who were number one on the hit parade to dancers for men's eyes only. For seven days and nights the good times rolled. While Xerxes and the good old boys were yukking it up, Queen Vashti decided to throw her own party for all the wives and girlfriends.

Even those remembering weeklong college celebrations can recall how even the best of parties begin to run out of steam toward the end. By day seven King Xerxes' shindig began to slow down a bit. He had dazzled the boys with his treasures and gold plates, goblets and even bathroom fixtures. Perusing his audience, the King needed a grand finale to take them over the top and it occurred to him that he had just the thing—his Queen. So he sent word to her that she should get the stylists busy with her make-up and hair and put on that hot number he had made for her by the world's most renowned seamstress before coming to him and his audience at the start of evening cocktails. When they see the Queen all decked out in her finest, those boys won't know what hit them. Xerxes smiled at the thought of it. When he got word that the Queen had declined his request and that the floor show was off, his smile turned to a frown and his blood pressure began to rise. He divorced her on the spot and sent word for her to pack her bags.

Vashti was well aware of her beauty. While she had used it to her advantage, she was much more than that. She had made it to the top and kept her self-respect. She was a queen, not just a pretty bauble to be oogled by a bunch of intoxicated buffoons. She knew her husband. She knew the risk involved. When he divorced her on the spot, she could not have been that surprised. She may well have already packed her bags just in case. Besides, she had noticed the way he lhad been looking at Esther. It was the same way he used to look at her. So be it. Vashti lost her royal position, but kept her dignity. One can imagine as the years passed, she thought more than once about what the look on Xerxes' face must have been when she refused his request. She may have smiled to herself each time she remembered.

LESSONS LEARNED AND OPPORTUNITIES MISSED

We know that looks can be deceiving and all that glitters isn't gold, and what seems a good deal can carry with it unintended consequences which can prove harmful to our well-being. Still, we are impressed by the gods of success and the many shiny objects the world dangles before us. If we are doing what we are called to do and being the kind of person God wants us to be, we can most likely handle whatever success or failure that comes our way. When instead of listening for God's call, we listen more closely to the siren voices of the world's promises, we tend to strive for success however we may define it rather than adhering to God's purposes.

Samson was blessed with a number of attributes, including his incredible strength. And his parents raised him to be a just and righteous leader of his people. Perhaps, he was too strong and too clever for his own good. Like we often do, when success came too easy, Samson may have begun to believe that his good fortune was due to his own prowess rather than being a gift from God. When that happens, it becomes easy enough to take a left turn when a right turn is required.

Samson missed many opportunities and wasted his talents for much of his life, but like all of us prodigal sons and daughters, in the end he remembered where he came from. He repented and in one last redemptive act of obedience made things right. Shakespeare had it right when he wrote, "All's well that ends well." And St. Paul didn't say he "won" the race. He said he "finished" the race. Even on the cross, Jesus said, "It is finished . . . or accomplished."

Susanna and Vashti, each in their own way, also finished the race set before them. They remained true to their inner worth and beauty even when their lives were put at risk. Their self-respect was more important to them than the opinions of others, including the courts and the King.

What the stories of these three persons offer us is that in many ways, life's journey is fragile and unpredictable. One can live a good and upright life well into adulthood and with one poor choice, destroy his or her reputation. It can be a matter of lust like with the two elderly judges, impulsiveness, pride and vanity as with Samson or in more modern parlance, an unethical or illegal business transaction. Whatever the circumstance, the years of good and upright behavior won't be what is remembered. That last act of deception, anger, or immorality resulting from vanity, insecurity or selfishness is what people will remember. When what others think of us or how they see us is more important than what God thinks about us, trouble and sorrow are sure to follow.

The good news is that no matter how big a mess we have made of our lives, through God's grace and mercy, redemption is possible. Like Samson, we can repent and pull down the pillars of our vanity and pride. We can become more like Vashti and Susanna and return to a place of self-respect. With the help of the Holy Spirit, we can begin to see others, especially the least of us, not as the world sees them, but through the eyes of Jesus. We can become more about humility than pride, reconciliation than retaliation, and service to others rather than service to ourselves. We can finally see with our spirit eyes what's on the inside, the intrinsic beauty and worth of all God's creation.

QUESTIONS FOR REFLECTION AND DISCUSSION

1. What are some examples of how our contemporary society worships physical appearance, celebrity and wealth?
2. How can such pressures affect our perceptions of ourselves as well as our health with emotional distress, including eating disorders?
3. If you had been a modern-day Samson, how do you think you would have handled yourself? What temptations might you find difficult to resist?
4. What about Susanna and Queen Vashti? Would you have risked your life to keep your honor and self-respect? Can you think of instances in today's world where husbands and wives have tolerated emotional abuse and infidelity in order to maintain status in the eyes of the world? On the other hand, what might some virtuous reasons be for staying in a difficult, unjust relationship?
5. What do you consider the most important lesson the story of Samson offers us to reflect upon?

7

A Liberated Woman

Luke 13:31–35; 23:1–12
Matthew 14:1–12
John 20:1–18

> "Being a woman is a terribly difficult trade,
> since it consists principally of dealing with men."
>
> JOSEPH CONRAD

> "Women should remain at home, sit still, keep house,
> and bear and bring up children."
>
> MARTIN LUTHER

> "Whatever women do, they must do twice as well as men
> to be thought half as good. Luckily, this is not difficult."
>
> CHARLOTTE WHITTEN

IDEAS AND ORGANIZATIONS RELATED to women's liberation have been in place for a number of years. The nature of conflicting views regarding the liberation of women can be seen in the quotes that start this chapter. A woman's right to vote, to have access to advanced education and a choice in what profession she chooses and to be treated justly where domestic abuse and sexual assault have occurred, have involved long-term struggles, some which continue in contemporary society. Other more controversial issues like those surrounding abortion and a woman's right to choose, have been a lightening-rod for heated political and religious discourse, protest and even acts of violence. While modern controversies concerning what it means to be a liberated woman may be unique in some ways, the core issues have remained much the same throughout history.

When the Israelites escaped from Egypt in order to be free from bondage, they wandered throughout the Sinai plains for forty years. Their history was one of internal conflict and wars with other nation-tribes interspersed with times of relative peace and freedom. In addition to being taken into bondage by the Babylonians, Israel's suffering and despair also resulted from their wars with the Persians and King Cyrus. Finally, around 63 BC, Rome took control of Israel and the Northern and Southern Kingdoms. In some instances, they were carted off as slaves to the victor's lands while on other occasions they were enslaved in what had been their own land.

The two stories in this chapter occurred during New Testament times when the Romans were the invaders and oppressors. From time to time, the Israelites rebelled and struck back with local leaders assembling fighters and attacking the Romans. When such rebellions happened, the leaders were martyred, usually by brutal means such as crucifixion. The aftermath of such uprisings typically resulted in the Romans and their puppet governments tightening their grip.

Herodias and Mary Magdalene provide contrasting approaches to the tyranny of the Romans and the puppet rule of Herod Antipas, the tetrarch of Galilee. Herodias was in fact, part of the Roman oppression. She did what she could to support her insecure husband and maintain his and her position of status as well. There were few, if any, lengths she would not go to including having her daughter, Salome, ask for the head of John the Baptist. Mary Magdalene on the other hand was a positive force of nature. A close follower of Jesus, she became one of the leaders in the early church following Jesus' death and resurrection. While there remains some dispute regarding Mary's life, it is clear that she was a leader among women. She held a position of prominence with the disciples and helped finance them as they traveled and ministered throughout Galilee and Judea.

LIKE MOTHER, LIKE DAUGHTER

It wasn't easy being a woman in Jesus' time, especially a woman with high ambition and the intelligence to weave her way through the labyrinth of intrigue and politics of a royal court. Herodias, a granddaughter of Herod the Great, was originally married to one of his sons, Herod Philip. Intermarriage among royal families has been common throughout history inevitably with less than stellar genetic results. Herodias and Herod Philip had a daughter named Salome. One can imagine that for a time life was good for the two of them. Living in Rome, they enjoyed some degree of access to high society. While in Rome, Philip's half-brother, Herod Antipas, came to stay with them, a visit that turned into an affair. Why did it happen? Was she bored with her husband Philip who had been exiled and disinherited by his father, King Herod? Or was her choice based on a more calculated assessment that Philip's prospects were no longer promising? Perhaps, she and her husband's half-brother were attracted to each other and experienced something that resembled love to them. Whatever the reasons, she left her husband and along with her daughter, Salome, ran off with his half-brother, Herod Antipas.

In the high society of Galilee, the affair and resulting marriage of Herodias and Herod Antipas while against the law, was taken more as a juicy morsel of gossip than a serious crime. While the royals and their intimate associates may have snickered about it, John the Baptist roared. He went public and ballistic over their infidelity and law-breaking.

A Liberated Woman

Through a combination of intelligence, charm and shrewdness Herodias was able to cajole Herod Antipas into divorcing his wife and marry her. A weak and somewhat timid man, Antipas was also cunning which is perhaps, why Jesus referred to him as "that fox." A bold, ambitious wife seemed to suit the more reserved and cautious and insecure ruler. Of course, the consequences of Herodias's success included Herod Anitpas's ex-wife returning to her father whose tribe then declared war on Herod. More serious than tribal conflict were the mutterings of the Jewish people, who detested incestuous marriages such as Herod and Herodias's. Such unions were against the Law of Moses.

Then there was John the Baptist. His garments, diet and lifestyle were as wild as he was. A fearless, intimidating presence, he was immune to the maneuverings of Herodias. John the Baptist was as far from the influence of royalty as the east was from the west. Instead of whispering the sweet-nothings of royal wannabes, John gave Herod and Herodias a double-shot of hellfire and brimstone. He was a take-no-prisoners kind of man—repent and be baptized or perish along with the rest of the "brood of vipers" in the snake-pit you have created.

Herod Antipas being both a careful and cunning ruler, wanted to be rid of the prickly thorn that was John the Baptist who railed relentlessly like a broken record against him. Yet, he was also aware that his subjects adored John—subjects who might well engage in open rebellion should he harm the prophetic wild man. While such a possibility frightened Herod, it had a very different impact on Herodias. She came to hate John with a vengeance. Herod was a half-way man, one who was caught in the middle between the wrath of his wife and the wrath of his people. So he went half-way and put John in prison to appease his wife, but stopped short of what she really wanted—John's execution.

While as Paul suggests, a little wine might be good for the stomach, too much wine can too easily allow one to act on an ill-fated impulse. And so it was with Herod Antipas. After all it was his birthday or some other special occasion which included dining, dancing and the customary tradition of granting favors.

Unsteady from his third bottle of wine and abandoning himself to a leering imagination, Herod was enthralled by the suggestive undulations of his step-daughter Salome as she danced her magic before him. Most likely, Herodias kept a watchful eye at a discreet distance observing her daughter's movement, gyrations that resembled a mating call more than a dance. Perhaps, she thought to herself, "Good girl, Salome. Just like we practiced. In a man's world, a woman has to do what a woman has to do."

More than a little drunk and proud in a perverse way of the effect Salome had on himself and the other men present, Herod was in a bragging mood, one in which he granted his step-daughter anything she desired. We can only imagine the reaction of Herodias. Maybe, she bit tongue to keep from shouting in glee. In modern parlance, she thought, "game over." And what about her daughter, Salome? Did she have any motherly instincts toward her or was she simply a pawn in the game to be used toward a desired end? Who can say for sure what Herodias's true feelings were toward her daughter, but it seems clear enough that whatever she thought of Salome, it wasn't the traditional protective view that most mothers hold toward their daughters. Salome herself, seems not as ambitious as her mother and more than a little dependent on Herodias's approval. "What should I ask for?" was her question to her Mother, not realizing that she would be included in the infamy that resulted. What does seem clear is that she was intimately in touch with her sexuality and the impact it had on men. Perhaps, with a cold, calculating mother, she may have accepted attention from whomever offered it.

Herodias was given John the Baptist's head on a silver serving platter as though it was a prized entrée at a royal feast. Ironically, the game wasn't over. In fact, it was just beginning. It might well be that Herodias was not only responsible for John the Baptist's execution, but she could have also observed Jesus, mocked and beaten, as he was sent back to Pilate. In the mind of Herodias, driven by an ambitious lust for power, she would most likely have concluded that two threats to her husband's reign had been eliminated. Peace was at hand. Of course, that's not how life works out.

What goes around tends to come around. She and Herod Antipas got sideways with the new, neighboring ruler on the block, one Herod Agrippa who it turns out was intimate friends with the notorious Roman Emperor, Caligula. The long and short of it was that rumor suggests that she and her husband were banished to somewhere in Gaul where they were never heard from again. The cunning Queen and shrewd, insecure King who killed John the Baptist, had it in their power to save the life of Christ. Instead, they disappeared into the mists of history blind to the missed opportunities and folly their lives represented.

MARY MAGDALENE: FROM DESPAIR TO DELIVERANCE

Mary more than likely grew up in Magdala, a small town by the Sea of Galilee, a center for drying and salting fish. She probably had a relatively normal upbringing for a young, Jewish girl. At some point, she married and her husband appears to have been a man of some means. At some point, her marriage ended. It may have resulted from the death of her husband or he possibly could have divorced her for one reason or another, including her inability to give birth—especially to a male heir. Whatever the circumstance, at some point Mary began to suffer from serious emotional and psychological problems. Her mental and emotional suffering became so intense that she became dysfunctional. She was said to have been possessed of seven evil spirits. Then along came Jesus who healed her mind and spirit. The Gospel records the story of a Jewish girl whose gratitude was so great that she followed Jesus to the cross and beyond.

It is reported that Simon the Pharisee was indignant and repulsed that Jesus would let a woman like Mary wash and dry his feet with her hair. Jesus replied to the high-minded Simon that her sins were forgiven because she "loved much" unlike the Pharisee who loved little, but "judged much." Mary didn't have the ambition or means Herodias had, but neither did she have the cold, calculating heart.

Mary is mentioned in all four gospels in connection with five events: 1. Being healed by Jesus; 2. Following him along with other women and providing him and the disciples with substantial material support; 3. Being present at his crucifixion; and 4. Coming early to the tomb on Easter morning to anoint his body; and 5. Encountering the risen Christ

It is in the last two events that we see the clearest picture of what Mary had become from who she was, a woman liberated from despair and bathed in the love and courage Jesus offered her. Faithful is an understatement regarding Mary's devotion to Jesus. While most of the disciples were hiding in fear, she was present at the crucifixion and she watched as Jesus's broken body was placed in the tomb. While it was still dark, she hustled down to the tomb that first Sunday morning to anoint the body of Christ. The Gospel of John tells us that the risen Christ commanded her to go tell the others which earned her the title of "Apostle to the Apostles." Crying and lamenting on where the body of Jesus had been taken, someone she thought was a gardener approached her. She asked him where the body of her beloved had been taken so she could go there. Then he spoke her name, "Mary." When he said "Mary," it was like she was healed all over again. It was him! He was alive! She was alive again! Hurrying back to the disheartened disciples, she uttered what must have been the most profoundly joyous words she would ever speak for the rest of her life. "I have seen the Lord."

Mary, the one who bore him and Mary, the one who followed him, two women—one who gave birth to him and one he gave rebirth to. Following the ascension, Mary Magdalene became a leader in the early church. In a time and world that held little regard for women, a world where men often did as they pleased where women were concerned, Mary stands as a beacon of true liberation. Like women of today who often have to do twice as much to get have as much recognition, Mary carried on for the love of Jesus and the purpose of spreading the good news to women and men alike.

LESSONS LEARNED AND OPPORTUNITIES MISSED

Sometimes we can't see the forest for the trees. Born in privilege, but born in a man's world where women were subordinate and often powerless, Herodias was so busy trying to hold onto what she thought she had that she couldn't see what she didn't have. She could not see the truth of John the Baptist's message to her—a message that called for her and Herod's need to repent. Nor could Herodias consider the promise of the outsider Jesus' message of hope and salvation. What she saw as a threat was actually her key to deliverance. Raised in the intrigue and betrayal of the royal in-crowds, maybe she couldn't help herself. In a sense, it's a little hard to blame her. Perhaps, she was doomed from the start. Bright and ambitious, at some point she came to trust only in herself. The security and allure of power and royalty turned out to be a fool's errand. If she realized her folly at all, she realized it too late. Pride, intimidation, political maneuvering, and everything else that goes with such ambition in the end was lost to her. One wonders if she nibbled grapes as she watched them take Jesus away to stand before Pilate, wondering—maybe even a bit curious—about what all the fuss was about? Probably not.

Unlike Herodias who started out in royalty and ended up banished to a place of oblivion, Mary started out in a more common station in life. She descended into the abyss of despair only to be resurrected through the healing touch of Jesus to a new life. While Herodias was driven by fear and cunning, Mary, though beaten down and emotionally left for dead, chose love and hope. In the end, she is the one whose love for Jesus was greater than her fear. One woman trusted no one even as the opportunity for her salvation and a new life passed by her. The other trusted even in the dark as she hurried toward the uncertainty of the tomb, hoping against hope for more than she could ever have imagined.

Like Herodias, in spite of all our talk and professed beliefs, we tend to trust in the riches and power of this world rather than the world to come. We are inclined to worry more about an earthly supreme court than "the" eternal Supreme Judge. Our actions speak louder than our words. We want to be political and religious insiders and too often like the Pharisees of Jesus' time, we are more about "show and tell" than "see and do."

For those of us who have experienced the love of Christ, we are also a bit like Mary Magdalene. We become so hopeful and full of joy that when we turn our eyes and hearts toward him rather than the bright lights of the world's ambition, we are content in that knowledge alone. As a woman hopeless and full of despair, Mary was the "least of those" in her world. When she experienced the light of Jesus, she ran toward it with all she had. Although we try to straddle the fence of being in the world, but not of it, we are never successful and in the end, always pay the price one way or another. Instead, we should follow Mary as she ran toward the light.

QUESTIONS FOR REFLECTION AND DISCUSSION

1. Why do you think Herodias turned out the way that she did? What do you think you would have done in her place? Can you think of ways contemporary women of note and wealth may struggle with similar issues?

2. What role did Herod Antipas, a half-way man, play in the events that transpired? What kind of example did he set as a political leader and a father and husband? For men and women in power, what are the risks of maintaining fame and power at all costs?

3. Why is Mary Magdalene such an important figure in the New Testament?

4. What are some struggles she endured that contemporary women still face in one way or another?

5. In what ways does Mary Magdalene set a good example for us?

8

Making Choices at the Crossroads

Acts 5:1–9
Acts 9:10–19
Luke 17:11–19

> "People do not lack strength; they lack will."
>
> VICTOR HUGO

> "God is omnipotent—but powerless still
> To stop my heart from wishing what it will."
>
> ANGELUS SILESIUS

> "When you have to make a choice and don't make it,
> that is in itself a choice."
>
> WILLIAM JAMES

> "Often people ask how I manage to be happy despite having no arms or legs. The quick answer is I have a choice. I can be angry about not having limbs, or I can be grateful that I have a purpose. I chose gratitude."
>
> NICK VUJICIC

We find ourselves at crossroads throughout our lives. Which way do we go, right or left or straight ahead? Making choices requires commitment to the kind of attitude we want to have through the thick and thin of our lives. A problem with the idea of commitment is that we can be committed to this or that way doing things—acting in ways that can be hurtful or helpful. A committed Christian may declare war or peace in family relationships or on an international stage. The kind of commitment Jesus teaches us to have is one where we pay attention, act compassionately and possess discernment that relies on the guidance of the Holy Spirit. The committed seeker is not one who is above or below the human condition, but rather resides in the midst of it. Seeking God's will requires us to become immersed in his creation rather than withdraw from it—be in the world, but not of it. It may be less a matter of whether or not we lose our way than how time and again when we do, we find our way back. At the center of a committed life is the struggle for meaning and reconciliation. A powerful illustration of the Christian engaged in the human condition is St. Paul's conflicts. He is honest and forthright about his highs and lows as he forges ahead in his quest to spread the good news to all who will listen. He is clear about his struggles within and his actions without. He tells us how he doesn't do what he wants, but instead often does what he hates.

So on we go, trying to become more fully human and Christ-like in a world that can often be unforgiving and inhumane. We live with our contradictory emotions and choices as we stumble toward the truth of God's love. The temptations Jesus faced for forty days and nights in the desert foretell the temptations and crossroad choices we each will face throughout our lives.

THE TWO FACES OF ANANIAS

There are two Ananiases in the book of Acts and they were almost opposites of each other. The first Ananias can be found in Acts 5 where he sold a piece of property and with the consent of his wife, gave a portion of the profits to the apostles and kept the rest for himself.

In our world what he did seems reasonable, perhaps even generous, but in the world of the early Christians they shared whatever they had. Pooling their resources, they gave to each according to his or her need. Their communal society was based upon trust and generosity with each other. Ananias was well aware that he and his wife deceived the apostles and the community which they belonged to. Perhaps like us on occasion, he decided that as long as he helped the community why not help himself as well—none would be the wiser. We see this time and again throughout history as when Solomon eventually resorted to the practice of donating one for God and two for Solomon. It seems even easier in our modern world to rationalize and justify our lack of contribution to the church and other religious communities we are a part of both in terms of our money and time. After all, whose business is it what I give? It's between me and God. Indeed, it is between us and God and as has previously been stated, our choices always sooner or later have consequences. The consequences for Ananias and his wife's greed and deception came sooner rather than later.

Unfortunately for Ananias, Peter knew that the land Ananias had sold was worth far more than the monies he had brought to the community. When he confronted Ananias about what he had done with the words, "You did not lie to us, but to God," we are told that Ananias fell down and died. Was it shame, shock or embarrassment? While we cannot say for certain, Peter's stark condemnation no doubt was a traumatic revelation to the community and to Ananias himself, strong enough to result in his death. As if that wasn't bad enough, three hours later Ananias's wife, Sapphire, came looking for her husband. She too was confronted by Peter regarding the money she and her husband had received as payment for the land in question. When she lied about the price, Peter responded with even harsher words: "How is it that you have agreed together to test the spirit of the Lord? Look, the feet of those who have buried your husband are at the door, and they will carry you out, too" (Acts 5:9). It is recorded that upon hearing Peter's words,

Ananias's wife also fell down and died. The shock of losing her husband and her dignity and self-respect was apparently too much for her to bear. It is interesting how often a slight turn this way or that way off the path God has chosen for us can lead to disaster. We aren't told that Ananias and Sapphire kept all the money or even most of it, but simply that they made a choice to award themselves an unauthorized commission. That it would lead to their deaths had to be the last thing on either of their minds.

There is also another Ananias in the book of Acts whose story ended quite differently. We know that he was a disciple in Damascus, perhaps even the leader of the Christian community located there. The Lord spoke to him in a vision and gave him instructions to go look for a man of Tarsus named Saul.

First, can you imagine Christ coming to one of us in a vision and calling us by name—Joe, Tom, Susan or Margie? What would our reaction be? Would we run for our lives, hide or possibly faint? When God called out, "Ananias," Ananias's reply was "Here I am Lord." So far, so good. Then Christ proceeded to tell him to go and look for Saul of Tarsus and when he found him to lay his hands on him so that his sight might be restored. Who? Yes, that Saul of Tarsus. While Ananias was a man of faith and courage who readily answered when God called his name he could not help but give voice to the question—"Are you sure you want to help this Saul?" He went on to make his case to the Lord by elaborating on the evil Saul had wrought and the persecution of the followers of Christ he had pursued with relish. It was well-known among early Christians that Saul encouraged and watched the stoning of the apostle, Stephen. In Ananias's mind, the blindness of Saul was a gift to his brethren who were being persecuted, not an affliction to be healed. The Lord, however, turned aside his complaint and instructed Ananias to do as he was told with the words, "Go, for he is an instrument whom I have chosen to bring my name before Gentiles and kings and before the people of Israel." The Lord said go so Ananias went.

Ananias entered the house where Saul was and laid his hands on him and said, "Brother, Saul, the Lord Jesus who appeared to you on your way here has sent me so that you may regain your sight and be filled with the Holy Spirit" (Acts 9:17). And immediately, as the passage goes, "something like scales fell from his eyes, and his sight was restored." When Saul rose, his baptism by Ananias was an essential part of his transformation from Saul the persecutor to Paul, the persecuted for the sake of the good news of Jesus Christ. After taking some food and regaining his strength, he became a zealot for Christ. Because Ananias made a choice contrary to his own preference and instincts in order to do what the Lord instructed him, Saul was able to become Paul.

ONE TURNED BACK: THE RESPONSE OF A GRATEFUL HEART

Besides the two Ananiases there is another example of "making choices at the crossroads." What sort of choice do we make in response to healing be it emotional, physical, spiritual or as is usually the case, some combination of the three? What do we do when what's lost is found—the cancer treatment is successful, the marriage is restored or the job we desperately seek is offered to us? Do we count it as good luck or fortune? Do we attribute the hoped for outcome to science, our own talents and perseverance? Perhaps, we say a small prayer of thanks before we move on to plot our next move?

The story goes that Jesus was on his way to Jerusalem when he was going through a region between Samaria and Galilee. As he entered a certain village, ten lepers approached him while keeping their distance as was required by custom and tradition. They lived in an isolated house near the entrance to the village from which they would come out to beg to those who passed by. They called out to Jesus, "Master, have mercy on us." Jesus stopped and told them to go and present themselves to the priests. They did as they were told and to their amazement found that as they went on their way, they were healed.

Of the ten lepers who were healed, only one, a Samaritan, turned back. He returned to Jesus praising God in a loud voice.

When he came to where Jesus was, he prostrated himself at the Master's feet and thanked him. Jesus' response was telling: "Were not ten made clean, but the other nine, where are they? Was none of them found to return and give praise to God except this foreigner" (Luke 17:17–18)? Then Jesus told the one who had returned with heart full of gratitude to rise and be on his way—that his faith had made him well.

One man was grateful for his healing and the one who healed him; the other nine may have felt some degree of gratitude, but not for the source from which their healing came. Are we more like the one who turned back or the nine who didn't? We lead busy lives and while we may not always know where we are going, we are usually in a hurry to get there. It's not that we wouldn't have appreciated the one who healed us, it's just that we have a schedule to keep and more to do than there are hours in the day. Perhaps, we can say a prayer of thanks when we go to church next Sunday.

It is also somewhat ironic, that with his parables like "The Good Samaritan" and other examples, Jesus typically points out that it is often the "least of those" rather than the well-healed members of the religious establishment that respond to his ministry and healing. A humble heart, not a proud spirit, is what gives us the "eyes to see" and the "ears to hear."

LESSONS LEARNED AND OPPORTUNITIES MISSED

It is easy enough for us to confuse our perceptions with God's reality. Good experiences and bad, we are raised in an environment that shapes how we look at the world and the people in it. Preferences, biases, and even prejudice are part of the stew that becomes our personality. Throw in a dose of fear and insecurity and we end up with a man or a woman, husband or wife, who looks for someone or something to believe in—a secure anchor in an uncertain world. And although we may find that anchor in Jesus Christ, we still tend to wander off and reach for what glitters in the distance. Spiritually speaking, we are all attention-deficit-disordered (ADD).

The first Ananias decided to pull a fast one and cut himself a taste of the profits from the sale of the land. After all, he did all the work. Shouldn't he be entitled to at least a small commission for his efforts? Besides, nobody needs to know. Who would be the wiser? We are all familiar with the verse that asks us the timeless question concerning what does it profit us if we gain the whole world, but lose our soul? Poor Ananias couldn't resist touching the hot stove of greed which resulted in him losing his life and his soul for a bit of personal profit. Greed can do to that to a person. As one of the authors told his Pastor in a conversation they had that the "good news" was that no matter what situation we find ourselves in, God is there with us. The "bad news"—no matter what situation we find ourselves in, God is there with us. In one way or another, at some time in our lives, we have all experienced the shame and disappointment of being caught with our hand in the proverbial cookie jar. Integrity and respect are earned through a lifetime of choices. They cannot be bought. For Christians those choices are best made under the guidance of the Holy Spirit.

Like Jonah before him, the second Ananias did not want to obey God's instructions. To help Saul of Tarsus, a persecutor and murderer of Christians was in his mind, too much to ask. He didn't want to help Saul, but he did it anyway. Men of a lesser faith and commitment may have faltered in responding to Ananias's vision, but his trust in Jesus led to his obedience even when it didn't make sense to him.

A lesson we can take from the example of the faithful Ananias is that more often than not, we don't know what is best for ourselves, much less anyone else. It is through the guidance of the Holy Spirit that we can do what needs to be done even when we cannot clearly see the way.

When we consider the example of the ten lepers, we might ask ourselves why are some people, including us at times, so ungrateful? Some folks may in general simply have a negative attitude toward life. They always tend to see the cup as half empty rather than half full. Others may, like the nine lepers, be so busy on their way to somewhere else that they don't pay attention to what they should be grateful for. Some may even feel a measure of gratitude for this or that action someone has taken on their behalf, but simply never get around to expressing their appreciation with a note or phone call. In fact, we all have regrets regarding what we intended to do, but didn't act on until it was too late.

Both of the authors have spent their vocation teaching students. In a sense, they were our "academic" children and some have remained our friends throughout the years—many of them now teachers themselves. We have rejoiced in their successes and suffered with them through their losses. Their expressions of gratitude to us and ours to them have given great meaning to our lives. Several years ago, one of the authors received an email from a former student who referred to the account of the leper who returned with a grateful heart, noting that he was the one returning to thank his teacher for what he had meant to him when he was a student.

The lesson of the ten lepers centers upon the "gratitude" of the one who was healed, not his "pride" in being healed. Grateful for, not proud of, is the difference between a humble heart and one of the seven deadly sins. Of course, we are proud of our children and grandchildren in a sense, but more than that, we are grateful for who they have become and the blessings God has bestowed upon them and us.

One of the authors who is also a minister learned a profound lesson in grace and gratitude from a ten year-old girl who was dying of cancer. Every time he would visit her, she would be upbeat, sharing with him what was good about her life. She always seemed to perceive the positive, regardless of the challenges of her day. On one occasion, she sensed the young minister was not having a good day and asked him to share with her what was bothering him. She proceeded to preach a sermon of sorts about what was special about life and how she was grateful for so much. She concluded that perhaps her life would be short (she died the next year), but that she was still grateful for the experiences and opportunities she had been blessed with. She said that many people had touched her and she hoped that the young minister had touched others as well. In an emotional moment, the young minister told her that she had deeply touched his life and that regardless of how long he would live, she would go with him—and she has.

In the end, we are grateful then for being loved and for being able to love; for what we have learned from the harm that we have caused and the harm that has been done to us; for the simple pleasures of a good meal and a warm fire; and most of all, for the love that surrounds us from the One who created us for now and ever more.

QUESTIONS FOR REFLECTION AND DISCUSSION

1. Can you think of choices you have made at crossroads in your life that you have regretted? What did you learn from such experiences?

2. Compare the selfishness, greed and deceptiveness of the first Ananias with the trust and obedience with the second Ananias. Are there ways in which we possess the weaknesses of the first Ananias? What does the example of the second Ananias teach us?

3. Have you ever felt you should do something you didn't want to do—reach out to someone you didn't particularly like or apologize to someone you felt was more responsible than you were for the harm that was caused in your relationship with them?

4. Is gratitude something that grows and matures or is someone born with gratitude?

5. What are some ways pride can undermine gratitude? Make a list of what you are most grateful for in your life? How does your list match up with what you spend most of your time and money on?

9

Embracing Scars
The Book of Job
Luke 10:25–37

> "The greatest pain is the one you can't tell others about."
> **PROVERB**

> "We hand folks over to God's mercy and show none ourselves."
> **GEORGE ELIOT**

> "I could work as much as a man. . . . and bear the lash as well . . . And I have borne 13 children—13 children! . . . and seen most all of 'em sold off into slavery, and when I cried out with a mother's grief, none but Jesus heard me!"
> **SOJOURNER TRUTH, FORMER SLAVE**

> "Have courage for the great sorrows of life, and patience for the small ones. And when you have . . . accomplished your daily task, go to sleep in peace. God is awake."
> **VICTOR HUGO**

EMBRACING SCARS

WE ALL EXPERIENCE PAIN and disappointment both given and received—and we have the scars and regrets as a result. When we were young and inexperienced, we were often full of pride and ambition whether looking forward to the vocation or the romantic interest we wanted to pursue. We may have moved head-long with a no-holds-barred approach to what we desired. An interesting irony is that while at that point in life, we had for the most part, experienced nothing, we often came to the point that we pretty much knew everything. We were in a hurry to get ahead, to get to wherever we thought we needed to go. And get there we did, usually in pieces. Then and now, speeding down the highway of life without a map or brakes tends to result in one sort of a crash or another.

Brokenness is an essential part of the human condition and experience. A broken heart from a love gone wrong that was supposed to last forever. A broken body resulting from an illness or injury. A broken mind where one's burden becomes greater than the capacity to bear it. Brokenness from within or brokenness from without can over time fill us with doubt and despair.

Our times of suffering are marked by scars made visible and more often than not, hidden from others and the face that looks back at us each day in the mirror of our lives. As the proverb at the beginning of this chapter reminds us: "The greatest pain is the one you can't tell others about." We live in an age where we hide from our age and the scars that go with it—some well-earned through sacrifice and service and others unwanted and undeserved. Our scars mark both our times of suffering and our times of resolve and perseverance. We can only show compassion and empathy for others in their times of suffering to the extent we have faced and come to grips with our own despair and dark nights of the soul.

SOMETIMES A GOOD MAN COMES IN LAST

When something bad happens to a bad person, it is easy enough to consider such an outcome to be a just reward, but when catastrophe hits someone we consider to be a good and moral person we are at a loss regarding what to think or say.

The story of Job is the archetypal confrontation of good and evil within the context of suffering. We are told that Job was "blameless and upright, one who feared God and turned away from evil." In addition, he was one of the wealthiest and most successful men around. A good, God-fearing man who was moral and compassionate—what more could one ask for or expect? Given the religious tradition of his day, one might assume that such a life well-lived would result in a healthy and prosperous existence. But as we know, that didn't turn out to be the case. In a single day Job lost it all. His livestock were stolen or burned up by a lightning strike. His workers were killed and a devastating storm destroyed the house along with his sons and daughters who were celebrating inside. And that was just the first part of the one-two punch. After experiencing that whirlwind of destruction, in short order Job became afflicted with leprosy. It was more than any man could take. Job cursed the day he was born. He wanted to die, but he kept on living if one could call it that. As if that wasn't enough, instead of comforting him, his wife perhaps herself experiencing the depths of despair over the loss of their children, told him to curse God and kill himself. Job's wife could have been a glass half-empty, the good times can't last kind of person or maybe she wasn't. Whatever the case, the tidal wave of misfortune that overtook her and her family could undo the strongest of women. Still, her response to her husband's suffering is telling. Rather than cleaving to him at his lowest point, she abandoned him emotionally, something even when his good fortune was later restored, he couldn't help but remember.

There were also his so-called friends who pestered him with the notion that he must be guilty of some secret sin. As the old saying goes, "with friends like that, who needs enemies." Pondering Job's sudden and overwhelming loss and suffering and the lack of support and consolation from those closest to him, helps us better understand why some in similar situations take their lives. But Job was no ordinary man. Somehow, someway, Job didn't quit.

Covered with sores and the memories of his good life disappearing faster than a hot summer's morning mist, he gathered up what was left of himself. He found his voice and protested the injustice of it all. In a very real sense, he called God out. Either he was guilty or God wasn't just.

History is full of Jobs. The ruins of Auschwitz's concentration camp ovens, the starving, dazed eyes of wounded refugee children in the midst of senseless wars, the homeless veteran with a thousand yard stare sitting on a sidewalk grate on a freezing January night as well as countless other victims of injustice and cruelty, cry out in silence for an accounting. Who should be called to account? The terrorist who pulls the trigger, the politicians who start a war for all the wrong reasons or God himself? Or should an accounting also include the rest of us who stood by, full of apathy, self-interest or even fear while others different from us suffered the pain of loss through floods and famine or the injustices of cruelty at the hands of those more powerful than them. What was the greatest injustice Job suffered, the loss of his property and children or the lack of support from his wife and friends?

Job, the leper, rose from the ashes with what was left of his body. He didn't give up or give in. He turned a deaf ear to his wife and his babbling acquaintances and talked instead, directly to God. Job remembered—remembered when his life had been blessed and when he was a whole man—when God was with him and when he was with God. And he asked why? Why? Where was God now?

And then God answered Job. When God breathed his answer on Job, it took Job's breath away. It was both heard and experienced through every pore and fiber of Job's body. Job reverberated like a tuning fork in the presence of God's revelation. "Prepare yourself . . . I will question you, and you shall answer me . . . Where were you when I laid the foundations of the earth? . . . Have you commanded the morning since your days began? . . . Have you entered the springs of the sea? . . . Can you lift your voice to the clouds?" And that was just the start of God's response, a response that called Job to answer for himself, a call that left Job a cowering puddle of nerves, wondering if perhaps, he had said too much. Job got humble in a hurry and acknowledged his smallness and God's greatness. We can imagine Job prostrate, face to the ground, sputtering, "I will say no more." Maybe, it was Job's way of crying "uncle," but God wasn't through with him yet.

When God had finally finished what he had come to say, Job had become transformed. He no longer quivered in fear, but now in awe, bathed in the transcendent majesty of God's presence.

The "why" of it all no longer mattered. He had experienced the unbearable light of God's presence and the unimaginable wonder of his being. He had heard and seen the One who was everything and then some. What was there left for him to do, but to "repent in dust and ashes."

Still, God wasn't through with him for he is also the God who embraces scars and gives second chances. Job did not give up even when he most felt like it. And even when he protested the injustice of it all most loudly, he refused to deny God by proclaiming, "Even if he slay me, yet will I love him." When Job called out, God came, not at the end of Job's suffering, but in the middle of it with the gift as terrible and merciful as it was, of himself.

WHO IS MY NEIGHBOR?

The story of the Good Samaritan is well-known. The road from Jerusalem to Jericho was a dangerous thoroughfare known as "The Bloody Pass" because of frequent attacks by robbers and bandits. A badly beaten man lay motionless on the ground. The priest and Levite saw him lying there. They may have stopped to size up the situation. Was he dead or alive? Or was he a decoy, hoping to lure potential victims to his aid so that his fellow bandits could fall upon them and take whatever they had of value before leaving them beaten and bloody—even worse, dead. We don't know what went through their minds or what their final assessment was. Maybe they were afraid. Maybe they were late for an important church or temple meeting. Maybe they even said a prayer for the hapless victim before continuing on their way. What we do know is that these two religious leaders for whatever reason, left him lying where he was in an unconscious heap as they quickened their pace toward Jericho.

At some point, a Samaritan saw the same man in the same place. Perhaps, he also kept his distance at first and carefully considered the situation. He may even have been tempted to move along as well. Instead, he felt compassion and chose not to. He treated the injured man's wounds as best he could before placing him on his animal. He walked while the beaten man rode. In Jericho, he found a room at an inn where the victim could recuperate. Paying in advance, the Samaritan instructed the inn keeper to provide whatever assistance was needed and that he would reimburse him for any additional costs.

When Jesus asked the expert in the law whose initial question was about what was required of him to inherit eternal life, which one of the three men showed mercy to the victim, the answer was obvious. The lawyer responded, "He who showed mercy on him." Then Jesus replied, "Go and do likewise." It is interesting that it was a lawyer who was focused on the "requirements"—what did he have to "do?" Like the lawyer, when it comes to embracing the scars and needs of the least of those among us, we are often more interested in the technical—minimal—requirements required for us to meet our spiritual obligations. Jesus' illustration was less about the legally acceptable requirements and more about the deeper moral motivation—about one's attitude and heart for compassion and action. And of course, the irony of the two men committed to a religious vocation who chose not to intervene is not lost on us when compared to the one from a tribe despised by their religious establishment who did choose to stop and help, going the extra mile to see that the wounded man was taken care of. The New Testament provides ample examples of instances where the "least likely" rather than the "most likely" step up to make a difference. The tax collector, the young boy with a few loaves and fishes and many others remind us that too often the more we have, the less we are willing to do. Perhaps, the poor and needy best understand how it feels to be poor and needy.

LESSONS LEARNED AND OPPORTUNITIES MISSED

Our scars, inner and outer, physical and emotional, remind us first, of wounds we have experienced and may still be suffering from and second, wounds we have also survived and even on occasion, grown from. Some of us, like Job, have had the rug suddenly pulled out from under us. Being fired from a job we thought was secure, experiencing divorce from a marriage that we thought was forever, or receiving a diagnosis of a terminal illness in the prime of our life, can all take away our equilibrium and sense of purpose. We may want to turn out the lights and curl up in a ball. Sometimes we choose drugs, alcohol, food or other destructive life choices as forms of self-medication. Anything to dull the pain. And too often, the wounds are too fresh and the scars too deep which can lead some of us to give up hope and consider taking our lives.

Job is the poster child for someone caught in the middle of relentless suffering and disappointment. A catastrophic whirlwind sucked him in and then spit him out. Covered with painful and oozing sores, his children dead, his livelihood gone and his wife and friends insensitive to his pain and sorrow, Job somehow still found a way to call out to the one who created him. Perhaps, the victim of robbers on the Jericho road also called out for help. Help . . . help, he may have called out to anyone and everyone in a hoarse whisper. And help came to each of them, one in the form of a man—a Samaritan—and the other in the form of God himself.

Even when Job, suffering from leprosy and abandoned by those closest to him, was at his wit's end or the bloodied and broken victim on the road to Jericho was given up for dead, God was near. And also, when Job's wife told him to curse God and die and his friends offered judgment and rationalizations rather than solace and encouragement, God was near. God was also present when the priest and the Levite looked the other way as they quickened their pace toward Jericho. God is also there with us—only a whisper away—when we think no one is looking. He is there in our darkest times when our wounds both visible and invisible are deepest. And we don't have to run the gauntlet of our sorrow alone to earn God's grace. He doesn't come to us at the end of our suffering. When we call out to him, he meets us wherever we are with the gift of himself.

QUESTIONS FOR REFLECTION AND DISCUSSION

1. Can you remember emotional scars you have received in your life? Can you remember scars you have given others?
2. What are some ways we try to carry or hide our scars?
3. What lessons does Job offer us regarding how we can embrace our scars?
4. Mother Teresa when asked how she could love and minister to the dead and dying on the streets of Calcutta, she responded that when she looked at them, she saw "Christ in a distressing disguise." In what ways did the Samaritan embody her sentiment?
5. Do you recall times when like the priest and the Levite, you have chosen not to provide help to someone you knew was in need? What lessons can we learn from the times we haven't given a cup of cool water or helped the least of those around us?

10

The Freedom to Forgive
Matthew 18:21–35
Acts 6:8
Genesis 37

> "Everyone says forgiveness is a lovely idea,
> until they have something to forgive."
>
> C.S. Lewis

> "In ordinary life we hardly realize that we receive a great deal more than we give, and that it is only with gratitude that life becomes rich. It is very easy to overestimate the importance of our own achievements in comparison with what we owe others."
>
> Dietrich Bonhoeffer

> "We must learn to regard people less in the light of what they do or omit to do and more in light of what they suffer."
>
> Dietrich Bonhoeffer

God's Scoundrels and Misfits

> "What a man does here and now with holy intent is no less important, no less true—being a . . . link with Divine Being—than the life in the world to come."
>
> Martin Buber

In today's world, forgiveness seems to be an idea much like owning a Bible—it's nice to have a copy of the Good Book handy and perhaps, have a framed forgiveness saying hanging on the wall for friends to see. Both have become more of a Sunday morning fashion accessory than something we actually take to heart. In a world where slander and hate speak have become acceptable, we hear people screaming epithets at each other and threatening harm, even physical violence over everything from a parking space taken at the mall to what this or that politician has tweeted about his or her opponent. Forgiveness as in forgiveness of financial debt has become a legal negotiation or strategy as in bankruptcy proceedings rather than a moral mandate taught by none other than Christ himself. Seventy times seven is not about money, but about the spiritual practice required by those who profess to follow Jesus. It is not an easy practice to follow, especially when we hear leaders proclaim that they don't get mad, they get even. The contemporary perversion of Jesus' admonition to his disciples isn't to forgive someone seventy times seven, but instead to retaliate, to seek retribution. Not an eye for an eye, but both eyes, and an ear and maybe a limb or two. That will teach them. It is interesting that when we are the victim of emotional or physical or financial harm, we want justice—punishment and retribution. However, when we are the offender, the one who has betrayed our friend's trust or for that matter the law, we want forgiveness and reconciliation—a second chance.

Throughout our lives when hurt and forgiveness come front and center, we always find ourselves at a crossroads. It is part of the great mystery of human nature that some seem to have a forgiving nature while others can't seem to let go of past injustices, real or imagined. Psychological and sociological explanations abound regarding the environment one is raised in, especially family dynamics surrounding the childhood years. Still, there are more questions than answers regarding why some folks insist on locking themselves in the prison of hard hearts and bitterness while others embrace the sweet spirit of forgiveness—even those who are victims of terrible child abuse and other horrific acts of violence.

THE SERVANT WITH THE DOUBLE STANDARD

Have you ever noticed that the people who are the most excited when they gain some advantage or profit at the expense of someone else, are also the ones who protest the loudest when they, themselves are taken advantage of? Such folks may even take great pride in pulling a fast one that would make the face of an unethical used car salesman turn red. These are often the same people that feign great relief and gratitude when their debts or other wrongs are forgiven. Their exaggerated praise to a forgiving benefactor may be appreciated only in the most superficial sense or worse, mask a kind of secret criminal pride of "getting away with one."

When Peter queried Jesus on what was the proper or legal requirement regarding forgiveness, the Master's response shattered the conventional etiquette surrounding what it meant to forgive someone—not three times or even seven times, but seventy times seven. Jesus followed his instruction with a parable about an unforgiving servant:

It was time to settle accounts and the Internal Revenue Service was working overtime. The King wanted what was due him. A fellow was brought before him who owed the King ten thousand talents or more than a million dollars in today's currency. Bankruptcy in the King's land was more severe than in our time. The King decreed that the debtor along with his wife and children be sold in order to pay the debt.

We are told that the servant prostrated himself before the King and pleaded for patience and mercy—that he would repay the debt he owed. The King's response was more than anyone in such a situation could have hoped for in a thousand years! Not only did his Master show compassion, but in fact, forgave him his debt. There must have been quite a family celebration following the King's verdict of mercy and forgiveness.

Unfortunately, that's not where the story ends. Perhaps, the servant like many of us, felt his big break was deserved or maybe he even felt a bit of satisfaction that he had pulled one over on the King himself. Whatever his thoughts were, it didn't take him long to locate one of his fellow servants who owed him several hundred dollars. Apparently none of the King's compassion rubbed off on him because he grabbed the one indebted to him by the throat and ignored the poor man's pleas for patience and mercy. Instead, he had him thrown into prison until the debt was paid in full. Needless to say, his actions didn't sit well with his fellow servants and they reported him to their Master. The unforgiving servant was obviously not the brightest bulb among the servants or he might have realized the folly and risks associated with the choices he made. We see those same characteristics today among folks who feel entitled and act arrogantly. It reminds one of the quote attributed to Marie Attoinette in reference to peasants during a time of hardship in France when she is purported to have said, "Let them eat cake."

When the hard-hearted servant was brought before the King, the time for small talk was over. No doubt, he pleaded again for mercy—just one more chance, but this time his plea fell on deaf ears. This time he was turned over to the torturers in prison until his bill was paid. One might wonder if he shared a cell next to the fellow he had thrown in prison and whether or not the irony of it all was lost on either of them.

THE LITTLE BROTHER WHO COULD

Most of us are familiar with the story of Joseph and his brothers. Not only was he the youngest and closest to his father, Jacob, he also had dreams and visions that placed him above his brothers in the future—dreams that he readily shared with them. There is no evidence that Joseph had any malicious intent in sharing his revelations, but be that as it may, he also displayed a substantial deficit in the tactfulness department. His lack of a social filter and his special coat of many colors which he wore with pride continually fanned the flames of sibling rivalry among most of his older brothers. Bright and loquacious and wearing a carefully tailored sport coat while his brothers' fashions consisted of well-worn work clothes didn't sit well with them and over time, turned jealousy and envy into hatred. In the language of today, Joseph was part of a blended family and being the son of Rachel, his father's favorite wife, made him in turn, his father's favorite son, added to a seething cauldron of dysfunctional family relationships.

Jacob sent his youngest to check on the flock and his brothers and report back to him. Like many doting fathers, Jacob seems to have had little insight into how his unbridled affection for Joseph was impacting his other sons. When they saw him coming, they quickly plotted to do him in and like most mobs, they proved to be braver together than they would have been acting alone.

It is interesting that hastily planned acts of violence and mayhem often get ahead of themselves. Once they had thrown Joseph down into the dry well and set things in motion, some differences of opinion began to arise. What would they say to their father? How would they kill Joseph? What would their father's reaction be? It might not go as well for them as they hoped. Maybe Jacob would turn to them in the absence of Joseph, giving them the attention they yearned for or maybe he wouldn't and instead, blame them for not protecting their younger brother. While they wanted to be rid of him, did they really want to kill him and anyway, who would do the deed?

Back and forth they went and then the solution appeared out of the dust of a desert caravan. A young boy named Joseph enslaved in a faraway land, a coat smeared with goat's blood presented to a broken-hearted father and an uneasy alliance of complicit brothers would seem to point toward a sad and unhappy ending, but God's ways are not our ways. God's logic defies ours and his plans and outcomes are known only to him.

LESSONS LEARNED AND OPPORTUNITIES MISSED

The hard-hearted, unforgiving servant missed the opportunities his second chance offered and paid a terrible price. Although the focus is on Joseph, in a sense, both he and his brothers had second chances—Joseph's to shed his pride and self-importance and mature into a wise and compassionate leader and his brothers to express their regret and rejoice in one they thought dead who was alive. Each made his choice. One resulted in a family reunion which embodied reconciliation and thanksgiving while the other choice exchanged the emotional prison of an unforgiving heart with a literal prison his Master cast him into. Often, how we think and feel on the inside becomes a prelude to the choices we make and the consequences—good or bad—that follow.

Debts are owed by each of us, some financial and others, relational. The legal aspect of our financial obligations are usually clear enough. We often try to apply the more black and white elements of legal logic to relationship-based obligations and responsibilities. That's what Peter attempted in his conversation with Jesus. Jewish law required one who was harmed to forgive his offender three times. In hedging his bets about what the Master might say, Peter indicated that perhaps forgiving someone seven times was a more proper criterion. When Jesus replied seventy times seven, Peter was stunned, his legalistic focus and definition of forgiveness shattered. As contemporary Christians, we might consider how many times God has forgiven our indiscretions and betrayals as purported followers of Christ.

In the parable Jesus shared with his disciples, his point about the relational dimension of forgiveness is driven home. Initially, the servant's debt was cut and dried. Legally speaking, he either had the money owed his Master or he didn't. If the servant did not repay his debt at the appointed time, the legal consequences were that he and his family would be thrown into prison. Once the King responded compassionately to his plea for patience and mercy by forgiving his debt, the transaction between them became relational. Using Jesus' parable as an analogy for us as contemporary Christians, we can surmise a similar relational context. For example, if we seek forgiveness for all our sins both past, present and future by the grace of Christ who bore them on the cross on our behalf, how can we not forgive others for the hurt feelings and harm they have done to us? How can we be forgiven for *everything* we have done and not forgive others for *something* they have done? We might also consider that if we can't forgive others for the wrong they have done us, perhaps we can't conceive of being forgiven—even by Christ himself.

In a different way, Joseph became the scapegoat for his dysfunctional family. Yet, when he had the opportunity to retaliate against his brothers—an act of retribution that would have surely been justified, he instead like the father who rejoiced in the return of his prodigal son, embraced them in a spirit of forgiveness and love. Rabbi Harold Kushner once suggested that it was less important where suffering and mistreatment came from than where and what it leads to.

INTENTIONS AS CHOICES

There is a popular old saying that contends "the road to hell is paved with good intentions." The saying is only partly true. More accurately, the road to hell is paved with good intentions "not acted upon." Our intentions—good, bad or indifferent—are at the center of our will and decision-making. While experiencing the grace of Jesus Christ may assure us of eternal life in the world to come, the world we live in guarantees us nothing. Everyday hundreds of thousands of people go to work making plans for what they will do when the day's work is over who never return home. Heart attacks, car wrecks and other calamities unexpectedly claim them. There are also those who find themselves looking into the abyss of failure only to find themselves with a winning lottery ticket. Misfortune and good fortune come to each of us throughout our lives in one way or another.

One of the authors taught an ethics class where he required students to put themselves in the middle of an untenable dilemma. They had to choose "either" to be a victim that would be beaten within an inch of his or her life, suffering great injury that required a long and painful rehabilitation *or* be the offender who attacked them and would never be caught by law enforcement and be brought to justice. It is easy to imagine the students' consternation. Most didn't want to choose either roles, but in the end decided to be the offender since they would never be brought to justice. Of course, for those who had a conscience, they wouldn't truly get away with it because they would know what they had done and would carry it with them for the rest of their lives. A more profound teaching moment came from the response of a young coed who raised her hand and said given the choices, she would choose to be the victim. When her teacher asked her why, she replied "because only the victim has the power to forgive." It was an insight the teacher would never forget for while it is true that we can be humbled and learn from the harm we have caused another—even live a more mindful life as a result, we can't forgive ourselves—only the victim and God can forgive us.

While we do not control what life brings us, we do have a choice in how we respond. Our intentions demonstrate what we are committed to. If we continue to try to put our good intentions into action no matter what the circumstance is or what the outcome might be, we find that we may travel the uneven road of life toward mercy and forgiveness. We love because Jesus first loved us. We can forgive others for the harm they have done to us because Jesus first forgave the harm we have done to him.

QUESTIONS FOR REFLECTION AND DISCUSSION

1. It seems the longer we wait to apologize, the harder it is to do. Why is it so hard to apologize and ask for forgiveness for harm we have caused someone in a relationship?

2. When it comes to addressing wrongs, like the unforgiving servant, do we find that we tend to hold others to a higher standard than we do ourselves? What are some consequences of that kind of attitude?

3. Joseph had been terribly wronged by his brothers. Instead of forgiving their young brother for his immaturity and impetuousness, their anger and jealously resulted in them selling him into for all they knew a life-time of slavery or even worse. What characteristics and qualities did Joseph possess that enabled him to forgive and show mercy to his brothers and restore the wellbeing of his family?

4. As Christians in today's world where there seems to be so much fear, anger and violence, what are some ways we can be more like Joseph in reconciling and restoring broken relationships?

11

The Faithful One

Matthew 13:31–36
Matthew 16
Matthew 26:14–16

> "If we really believe in something,
> we have no choice but to go further."
> — GRAHAM GREENE

> "We must be broken into life."
> — CHARLES RAVEN

> "Broken bones well set become stronger."
> — ENGLISH PROVERB

> "Hell is truth seen too late . . ."
> — TRYON EDWARDS

THE FAITHFUL ONE

IN ONE WAY OR another, each of us may have a bit of Peter and Judas hidden in the recesses of our personality. There are occasions when we are faithful to what we believe even in the face of peer pressure and other challenges. There may be other times when we betray our spiritual and moral values, times when we remain silent and go along with prejudiced sentiments and demeaning jokes. In such instances, we rationalize our lack of response or inappropriate chuckles as "going along to get along." We may even experience a guilty after-thought or a taste of remorse, but if we practice silence in such situations, our spiritual conscience will eventually become desensitized to the harmful words and actions we choose to tolerate.

Judas Iscariot and Simon Peter both betrayed Jesus. Fearful and despairing, Peter succumbed to slandering his good name and even resorted to cursing him. Judas for whatever reason, went a step further and took payment for betraying Jesus' trust. In our own unique ways, we follow suit when we betray someone's good name and character by bearing false witness in a conversation or on the internet through malicious gossip. There are also countless innocent victims who have been betrayed by others for financial gain and profit. We only have to look at our society's recent history of financial fraud and scams—some which were perfectly legal, but clearly immoral and unethical—where investors lost everything. C.S. Lewis contended that there were essentially two laws of human nature: We know what we need to do and we don't do it. His point is well-taken and seems to succinctly identify our ongoing dilemma including the dark side of Peter and Judas that hides near the surface of our own collective psyche.

THE ROCK CROWS THREE TIMES

Simon Peter was a fisherman by trade who lived with his wife in Capernaum. Peter's mother-in-law and his brother, Andrew, lived with them. He and Andrew must have been reasonably successful, because they had their own fishing boat and were in business with James and John, the sons of Zebedee. Peter was a man's man. He may not have been as eloquent or as sophisticated as some of the other disciples, but you always knew where he stood. What you saw is what you got. Peter's passion for Jesus was also loud and clear and at times, more than a little impulsive.

In Matthew 13 when the disciples were caught in a horrific storm that threatened to capsize their boat, they were terrified. Jesus appeared at a distance walking on water. When Jesus said, "come," Peter went. While the other disciples cowered and clung to the sides of the boat, Peter climbed over the side and walked toward Jesus—until he took his eyes off Jesus and looked down. Although Jesus admonished him for his lack of faith after he rescued Peter from drowning, it is worth noting that it took faith and courage for him to even get out of the boat. We could ask the question: How many of us would have chosen to leave the boat and try to walk through the stormy waves to Jesus? Better yet, metaphorically speaking, how often do we choose to let go of whatever we are clinging to during one of our life's storms and try to make our way to Jesus when he beckons us to let go of our fear and come to him?

While Peter had a big heart and a big passion for Jesus, he also, like the rest of us, had an ego. When Jesus said that some people contended that he was John the Baptist or Elijah and asked the question: "Who do you say I am?" Peter answered without hesitation, "You are the Messiah, the son of the living God." Jesus replied that Peter was indeed blessed and possessed the kind of faith that he would build his church upon. A strong man, a strong faith, Peter, the rock—he was on a roll and perhaps, more than a little puffed up. We are reminded that pride always goes before the fall and Peter was about to be shaken to his core—but not just yet.

Peter unabashedly proclaimed his love and loyalty to the Master only to be told by Jesus that he would deny him not once or twice, but three times before the cock crowed three times. In Peter's mind Jesus' prediction didn't compute. No way. No how. In one Gospel's account, Peter even cut off the ear of one of the Temple guards who came to arrest Jesus. Yet, in spite of Peter's proclamations and denials, it happened just the way Jesus said it would happen. The result was that as far as Peter was concerned, the rock had crumbled. Yet, Jesus had another plan. He told a disbelieving Peter that he would pray for him and the wings of the Master's prayer brought hope to a broken and bewildered disciple. With Jesus' resurrection, all the broken pieces of the rock that had been Simon Peter were put back together again. Repentance, forgiveness and redemption restored Peter's purpose. Still, it is worth remembering that Peter like the rest of us, still had his ego which got in his way from time to time. We see in Acts 10 that he and Paul had their differences regarding including the Gentiles in the emerging Christian body. The good news for Peter and for us, is that Jesus left the best part of himself, the Holy Spirit, behind to help us on our way. When the Holy Spirit came to Peter and directed him to go to Cornelius, the Centurion, Peter's eyes were opened. He left his tradition behind and his ego at the door. He stayed with them, preaching the good news. The end result was that he baptized Cornelius, the Gentile, and his family.

IS IT I, LORD?

Throughout the centuries, the question has continually been raised. How could someone follow Jesus throughout his ministry, hear his words and see his deeds and then betray him? That is a question which is in many ways, difficult to answer. In comparison, we could also ask ourselves how could a life-long friend betray his or her compatriot for personal advantage or financial gain? Unfortunately, it happened then and it continues to happen now.

Judas at some point, perhaps on his way to Jerusalem for the Passover, decided to betray his Master. When Jesus and his disciples arrived in Jerusalem, Judas visited the chief priests, possibly even talking to Caiaphas himself. We don't know what they said to each other during the course of their conversation. What we do know is that their back and forth concluded with Judas agreeing to identify Jesus to the authorities for a sum of silver.

Judas stayed with Jesus and his fellow disciples and acted as if nothing was out of the ordinary. We know that on the night before he was arrested, Jesus broke bread and drank wine with his disciples. During their common meal, especially in celebration of Passover, there was a pledge and obligation of love and devotion. The disciples were shocked and dismayed to hear from their Master's own lips that one of them would betray him. Who was the traitor among them? Each of the disciples asked Jesus, "Is it I, Lord?" According to one of the Gospels, when Judas asked that question, Jesus replied, "You have said so" which in the Greek, means "yes." We aren't certain in what manner Jesus responded to Judas. Was his response whispered to Judas in an aside or was it clearly spoken in the presence of the others? Whatever the case, Judas was aware that Jesus knew what he planned to do.

On the ill-fated night, Judas left the disciples and joined the chief priests and their guards at a prearranged meeting place. Judas knew that Jesus would most likely go with a few chosen disciples to the Garden of Gethsemane. When the priests and guards came to the garden, Judas told them that the person he kissed was the one they wanted. Kissing itself was an innocent act, a typical greeting of a rabbi by his disciple. This kiss was different. This kiss was the kiss of death. So Judas did as he promised. He kissed Jesus who was arrested and taken into custody.

We return to the question: Why did Judas betray Jesus?

A frequent answer is that Judas did it for the love of money. The writers of Matthew and John depict Judas as a greedy and dishonest person. Perhaps, that could be part of his motivation. After all, he was the treasurer. He could have dipped into the ministry's funds from time to time for personal use. It wouldn't be the first or last time such a thing happened. It could also be argued that when he saw the ministry heading south, he felt it was time that he was finally compensated for his years of service. A problem with all of these reasons centers around the response of Judas "after" Christ was crucified. If he betrayed Jesus only for the money, why did he attempt to return the silver? Money as his only motivation doesn't really seem to offer a complete explanation of why he did what he did.

Another reason given for the course of action Judas chose to follow was that he was moved by the Spirit of violence and hatred.

A point can be made that while the rest of the disciples were Galileans, Judas himself was a Judean. Perhaps, he felt he was superior to the others and in the end became alienated from them. Luke answered the question by indicating that Satan entered into Judas.

Judas may have felt betrayed by Jesus. Iscariot means "leftwing Zealot." He may have believed like many other Israelites who hoped for the prophesied Messiah to throw off the yoke of Roman oppression and establish a new kingdom in the Davidic tradition. Jesus would be king and Judas would be a person of great importance and stature. Other scholars have suggested Judas might have been trying to force Jesus' hand, making him openly declare his Messiahship. If Jesus made such a proclamation, he and the other disciples could carry the day and the nation with them.

Some have also suggested is that Judas was confused like the other disciples and had lost faith in the Movement. A condition of his willingness to identify Jesus to the authorities may have included an understanding that Jesus would not be harmed—certainly not killed, but detained for a period of time and then released. Judas may have thought he might as well procure a bit of compensation on the side as a payment of sorts for his efforts to resolve what he may have considered a mounting crisis, dangerous to himself, the other disciples and even Jesus himself. Of course, Caiaphas would agree to Judas' terms. As a leading religious leader and politician, the difference between his promise and his actions were the difference between night and day. Regardless of Judas' motives, the evidence suggests he never believed his actions would actually lead to the crucifixion of Jesus. When he realized what he had done, he was horrified.

The trial took place. There is no evidence that Judas testified against Jesus or in any way participated in the trial. It is written that Judas returned the thirty pieces of silver to the high priests. They refused to accept the money whereupon Judas threw the money on the floor of the temple courts in disgust—disgust with the high priests and even more, with himself. We are told that he left the temple and went out and hung himself. That Judas saw the truth too late seems a fitting epilogue to the conclusion of his unfortunate life.

LESSONS LEARNED AND OPPORTUNITIES MISSED

Betrayal is nothing new in human experience. It happens every day on the highways and byways of life. Unfaithful is the flipside of the coin where faithful is engraved. Benedict Arnolds are found in the root causes of broken marriages, stolen retirements, corrupt governments, and dysfunctional societies. The same holds true for those of us who call ourselves Christians. Too often we choose a kind of blind faith in this or that religious or political demagogue rather than a more dynamic, seeking faith which relies on the guidance of the Holy Spirit. Blind faith promises us simplicity where everything is black or white. We feel safe in the herd. Don't question. Don't think for oneself. Circle the wagons. All will be well. Blind faith promises us security if only we will give up our freedom of thought and choice to one who knows better. Blind faith tends to be ten miles wide and three inches deep. Unfortunately, we may feel safest in the herd just before we go over the cliff. A dynamic, seeking faith follows the leading of the Holy Spirit, a leading that can make us uncomfortable as we move deeper into the forest of human suffering. It is less about feeling secure and well-fed and more about service to those in need and securing others so that they may be tethered to Christ. It is easy to be deceived and to deceive ourselves. The world's promises constantly beckon to us in the disguise of Christ, offering prosperity rather than sacrifice, pride rather than humility.

So we ask of ourselves throughout history as well as in our time, "Is it I, Lord?" The answer is, yes it is. We know of Christians who over the years have betrayed Christ when they cried "Master," but fought to retain the evils of slavery. If the anthem had been available to them, the Crusaders might have sung "Onward Christian Soldiers" as they marched through Arabia slaughtering Moslem women and children with abandon. After all, the Pope ordained it a "Holy War." We Christians burned and otherwise martyred other Christian sects like the Hugenots at the stake because they did not follow the same version of the faith that we did.

We continue to betray Christ whenever we choose to pursue privilege and self-interest at the expense of the poor who are largely invisible to us because we don't pay attention to what is going on around us. They don't live in our neighborhoods or go to our churches. A television political commentator recently opined that the poor don't have lobbyists. We betray the spiritual values Christ gave us and the leading of the Holy Spirit when we don't live up to what we profess—when we say one thing and practice something else.

What we can learn from Peter's betrayal is that a momentous failure cannot only be the end of something, but also the beginning of something else. Peter and Judas both felt remorse, regret and despair, but where Judas stopped at the crossroad of hopelessness and second chances, Peter reached for a chance at redemption in the hope that the God who was love also had a heart for forgiveness. Judas despaired of being forgiven. To his accountant's mind, it didn't add up and of course, in terms of justice, it didn't. The death he caused demanded retribution—a life for a life. If only he had waited, he would have found on that third morning, the dawning of second chances. Through the grace and mercy of the risen Christ, anything was possible, even the unforgivable could be forgiven when mercy held sway over justice. The hangman's noose demanded a verdict that unknown to Judas, the cross had already paid.

The story of Judas ended in the dark night of shadows and sorrow, but that was not to be the ending of Peter's story. Unlike Humpty Dumpty, the crumbled rock that was Peter was put back together again, made whole and stronger than before. Peter was still Peter. He surely continued to have his share of insecurities, but his pride was replaced by humility where real strength comes from. He still could be bull-headed, but he also possessed enough patience and forbearance to have the eyes to see and the ears to hear what the Holy Spirit revealed to him.

When we have betrayed someone as was true of Judas and Peter, we can't forgive ourselves of the harm we have done, but we can repent and try to make amends. Even if the one who was harmed doesn't choose to forgive us, we can learn from our mistakes. We can let the experience humble us and we can rest in the forgiveness of the one who created us and died in our place. We don't have to give up hope or give into guilt like Judas did. We can follow Peter's example and seek forgiveness, experience the grace of humility, and through the love of Christ, somehow become the better for it.

QUESTIONS FOR REFLECTION AND DISCUSSION

1. What does it mean to be faithful? Can we be "perfectly" faithful?
2. What does it cost to be faithful? What kinds of sacrifices are required?
3. Can you recall times when you were betrayed? When you betrayed someone else? What did you learn from such experiences?
4. What were the most important differences between Peter and Judas in the way they each responded to their acts of betrayal?
5. In what ways does our hope in the sustaining grace of Christ help us on our faith journey in today's world?

12

The Least Likely

Luke 19:1–10
John 3:1–21
Luke 18:9–14

> "A man is led the way he wishes to go."
> THE TALMUD

> "We could not seek God unless He were seeking us."
> THOMAS MERTON

> "... religions have the tendency to become ends in themselves and as it were, to put themselves in God's place, and, in fact, there is nothing that is so apt to obscure the face of God as a religion."
> MARTIN BUBER

> "I believe in the small way of doing things, one person at a time..."
> MOTHER TERESA

The Least Likely

MOST COMMUNITIES ARE TYPICALLY a mix of all kinds of people, vocations, life-styles and value systems. In a more intimate sense, a community is also known by both the best and worst of its members. Are folks friendly, helpful and in general, good neighbors or are they distant, self-absorbed, pretentious and contentious? On a more personal level, the same is to a large extent, true as well. Whether we realize it or not, most people see us for who and what we are—the good, the bad and the ugly. At times, we are our best selves. On other occasions, we are at our worst. Rich or poor, famous or anonymous, privileged or excluded, every person has his or her insecurities both apparent and hidden. The better others know us, the more they see.

When we look at others, our preferences and biases quickly surface. How do they look? Are they attractive or unattractive to our particular eye? Do they look successful or well on their way to the poorhouse? Do they look like me, speak like me and believe like me?

There were Pharisees and Sadducees like the high priest Caiaphas who slithered between religion and politics with ease, mixing the two into a kind of deceptive, pragmatic stew. Obsessed with religious rules and projecting a kind of sleight-of-hand appearance of virtue, he worked twenty-four/seven behind the scenes to maintain political power. There was also the Pharisee who was the exception to the rule—Nicodemus. Though perhaps, a bit naïve, he tended to look at the world around him through the prism of his heart rather than through the lens of a self-absorbed intellectual legalism. He was more about the spirit of the law than the letter of the law.

Like politicians in today's world, the Pharisees in the context of their time and traditions most likely hit the fried chicken circuit when their version of the fourth of July and other holy days rolled around. Working the crowd, waxing eloquent with noon-time prayers and blessings just a little too long for the hungry church folks, they tried to put their best foot forward. When a person once mentioned that he heard that one of the candidates running for office was a Christian, his friend replied that everyone was a

Christian around election time. Of course, what they did between elections would require much more scrutiny.

On the flip side of the proud, high-minded and long-winded Pharisees were the outcasts and despised ones. The forlorn publican uttering his desperate prayers, the widow with her mite and Zaccheus, the hated tax collector—the kind of people we look away from. Maybe, we say a quick prayer for them while at the same time feeling fortunate that we aren't in their shoes. We say the prayer, but we don't stop to help. And in the case of modern-day tax collectors like Zaccheus, we are inclined to view them as the enemy, worthy of heaping blame on them for all our grievances past, present and future.

PHARISEES AMONG US

Pride has always been a double-edged sword of sorts. We are proud of our accomplishments, our children and grandchildren, our football team, country and so forth. Like other emotions and sentiments, there is always an upside and downside to such notions. While there is nothing wrong with feeling good about one's achievements, family members and even the winning record of one's favorite sports team, we are also reminded that pride is one of the seven deadly sins and that pride always goes before the fall.

In Luke 18, there are two men who have come to pray. The first is a Pharisee. He stands apart from others, confident and aloof. The contents of his prayer extol what he perceives as his own personal virtues. He makes sure that everyone who is within ear-shot hears about all the vices he abstains from. He doesn't drink, smoke or hang around with those who do. From there, he puts a spotlight on his special piety and all the merit badges he has earned since childhood in that pursuit. He is a man above men who goes the extra mile, fasting more than Jewish law demands, giving a tithe even when it is not required. God-fearing and disciplined with a bellyful of self-righteousness, he thanks God that he is not like the rest of men. Exceeding the legal requirements of religious etiquette, the Pharisee looks heavenly with a wide, sparkling smile that only a chest-full of medals and ribbons could produce. If he had been a television evangelist, he would have worn a starched white linen suit with white patent leather shoes on his feet, both a sign of purity to his audience. Raising his arms upward, he would fervently offer to use some of his mighty excess prayer power to raise up to the Almighty, the afflictions of his viewers for healing—for a small donation, of course.

In contrast to the Pharisee, we have the Publican, a man who knew he had failed miserably in living out his religious and moral values. He didn't even dare lift his eyes toward heaven. He wasn't worthy. Bowed and broken, his utterance was more a cry than a prayer. "Lord, have mercy" was his one and only prayer. He was open to whatever scrap of mercy that might be thrown his way. The Publican was well aware of his sin, deceit, and wrongdoing. He could taste the bile of it in his mouth. While the Pharisee stood apart and looked down on lesser beings, the Publican prostrated himself in the middle of the muck that had become his life and out of the corner of his eye, looked up with a momentary glance, hoping for a small taste of grace.

What about death row confessions? What about the persons who have committed terrible deeds that have caused great harm and suffering? If such persons repent and open themselves to God's grace and forgiveness, are they also included in Christ's welcoming embrace? Can a stone-cold killer become a Saint? Can Saul of Tarsus who persecuted Christians and held the cloaks of those who stoned the disciple, Stephen, to death become Saint Paul, transformed by the grace of Jesus Christ? During the course of their vocations, the authors have dealt with prison inmates, including some who were also on death row for many years. While many who profess religion in prison may have ulterior motives, there are inmates who undergo genuine spiritual transformation and become a new being in Christ. The authors have observed instances where lives have in fact, been radically changed—where a bad man became a good man—a new person in Christ.

The sad irony of it all is that had such persons never done their terrible deeds, they may have muddled through their lives.

Instead, the crimes they committed drove them to a six by nine cell where in time, they came to face themselves and their sin. Humbled and broken, in their own way they were transformed through the grace of Christ from a Saul to a Paul.

THE FORGOTTEN WHO ARE REMEMBERED

Can we see the picture? The well-heeled members dressed in the latest fashions sit in reserved seats on the front row with plenty of jingle and jangle in their pockets. The pastor nods approvingly from his high perch next to the pulpit as they place their substantial contributions into the offering plate. Everyone attending the service know who they are. Some look on with admiration, hoping one day to emulate their success and move closer to the front while others look on with envy.

No one noticed the elderly woman sitting on the back row. Widowed and living in an efficiency apartment in public housing, she got by as best she could on her meager social security check. No one noticed when she placed the last of her savings into the offering plate—no one, but Jesus.

There are others. The woman who kissed Jesus' feet and washed them with her tears while Simon, the host, offered no kiss of greeting to the Master or to anoint his head with oil. The small boy with a few loaves of bread and a child's handful of fish offering all he had to Jesus who fed five thousand with what seemed practically speaking, to be an insignificant gift. Onesimus, the runaway slave who had the good fortune to meet Paul in prison and become like a son to him. There is also the thief on the cross being crucified next to Jesus. Don't forget about him. His was a wasted life, poorly turned and literally broken in body as well as spirit. By asking Jesus for a drop of mercy—to remember him when Jesus came into his own, it was just enough of a gesture and request for him to be given a ticket for the last train leaving town for glory while Jesus was still present in the flesh. And of course, there are always the children—Jesus always had time for the children. Perhaps, their innocence reminded him of his own and their trust was the place

THE LEAST LIKELY

where he felt most at home. Maybe in his eyes they were the closest thing to the kingdom of God he would see in this life. He said, "Let the children come to me." And we, like the children he welcomed with open arms, must come like he told Nicodemus to come—to be born again into a new being, a new life—if we are to find a seat on his train to salvation.

There were the widows and the innocents, the homeless and the hopeless that Jesus payed special attention to. But he also had a taste for the ones that didn't know they were homeless and hopeless. The ones like Zaccheus who had plenty of money, but few, if any, friends. He was a despised and feared tax collector, the kind of person his fair weather friends might have a drink with on the back porch if he was buying, but didn't want to be seen with him in public.

Zaccheus was a small man who in a manner of speaking, carried a big stick with "tax enforcer" engraved on it. Barely five feet tall, he was the most hated man in all of Jericho. He received the glares and mutterings of those who passed him by. A cat-call here and there and an occasional stream of spittle found its mark from someone in the crowd who he could never quite identify. As far as friends and social relationships went, Zaccheus's life was like someone who was always dressed up with no place to go.

As head tax collector for Rome, he might have been small in stature, but he was big in money and power at least on the local level. Zaccheus heard that Jesus was coming to town and for one reason or another, he wanted to take a look at the man everyone was talking about. He knew better than to try to work his way up front through the crowd for a better vantage point so he climbed up a sycamore tree. Sitting on the edge of a limb, Zaccheus got a good look at Jesus. Jesus also got a good look at him. When Jesus told him to come down from the tree, Zaccheus went. Of course, the folks who had come to see Jesus couldn't believe their eyes and ears. Why was Jesus spending the night with Zaccheus, their enemy, when there were so many "good people" he could have stayed with? What was the world coming to? On that particular day, the world in its best self—in all its righteousness was in fact, coming to Zaccheus.

Needless to say, Zaccheus was stunned and flabbergasted by the turn of events. The most honored teacher had chosen to dine and stay with the most despised man. Overwhelmed, the one who had spent his life pursuing riches became the champion of charity and restitution. Zaccheus promised to use fifty percent of his wealth to help the poor. Furthermore, he was committed to paying back, four to one, money he had unjustly taken from other citizens of Jericho. Zaccheus's transformation is reminiscent of the character of Ebeneezer Scrooge in Charles Dickens' *A Christmas Carol*. The difference was that Zaccheus wasn't visited by the Spirits of Christmas past, present, and future, but by the one who embodied the Holiest of all Spirits standing before him in the flesh.

Jesus opened the door to salvation, but Zaccheus still had to choose to walk through it. When he did, Jesus responded by saying, "Today salvation has come to this house." A life-long crook with a demeanor as small and petty as his stature—who would have ever thought such a thing was possible? Jesus punched Zaccheus' ticket and welcomed him aboard, behind Jacob, the con-artist and ahead of the thief on the cross. All seats were reserved. Zaccheus probably sat there more than a little unnerved by it all in the company of the widow with her mite sitting to his right and the martyr, Stephen, sitting to his left. Maybe what it all boils down to is that Jesus not only sees the least of those who are hopeless and alone, the ones the rest of us tend to ignore, but also the least of each of us that hides within. Smiling and confident to those who pass us on the street, we run, but can't hide from the fear and insecurities we hope others don't see. In the end, Jesus doesn't want to have anyone left behind. As long as we draw breath—as long as we see someone looking back at us from the bathroom mirror, seats on the train to salvation are still available. Jesus is calling "all aboard."

LESSONS LEARNED AND OPPORTUNITIES MISSED

There are several lessons we can learn from what we have examined in this chapter. The Pharisee praying in public reminds us that too often, we can become self-satisfied with what we perceive as our own righteousness and faith and feel morally and spiritually superior to others. We tend to judge ourselves by the worst of humanity, relieved that we are better than that, rather than by the best examples of compassion and lovingkindness. We are glad we don't run around on our spouses or abuse our children, but are we willing to make sacrifices for Jesus like Lottie Moon and Mother Teresa did? We don't mind marching in a group for Jesus and proudly wearing a tee shirt proclaiming our faith, but what do we do when we think no one is looking? We may display the Ten Commandments in our front yard, but do we live by them?

The Pharisees obsessively defended their religious traditions. They looked down on outsiders like the Samaritans and excluded anyone who challenged their rules and practices like Jesus did. They wanted to appear righteous and holy, but on the inside they focused on themselves—what was good for them, not what was God's will. They were more interested in acquiring and maintaining political power, even if it required them to endorse and cater to Roman authorities at the expense of staying true to their faith. A lesson for us today is when we ignore this or that political candidate's spiritual values and moral conduct in exchange for political power that we think is best for us materially, we are following the way of the world rather than the way of the Spirit. We only have to look at Old Testament prophets for guidance. Prophets like Jeremiah and John the Baptist knew they couldn't be God's messenger—the conscience of the kingdom—if they were on the payroll or in bed with the King.

We are also reminded that God is more likely to use the least among us to do his work. In fact, Jesus tells us "that as you do to the least of those, you do to me." Some think he is talking about the attitude one should have and act upon, but that isn't what he says.

He says, "As you *do* to them, you *do* to me." In other words, you won't find Jesus sitting on the fifty yard line at the Super Bowl, but you might find him with the homeless searching the dumpsters outside the stadium for something to eat. He won't be the first one to eat at the banquet's head table, but will either be serving the tables or cleaning up the kitchen with the hired help. He chooses to eat the leftovers with them.

In the end, Jesus is more interested in who we are on the inside than what we have, the service we give more than the service we receive. We can't tip our way to heaven. There aren't enough merit badges in the world to get our eternal tickets to salvation punched. When we see those around us, homeless and hopeless or well-dressed and hopeless, we are seeing the least of our brothers and sisters. With a humble and open heart through the grace of Jesus Christ, we can begin doing our part in reconciling a lost world to his promise of redemption.

QUESTIONS FOR REFLECTION AND DISCUSSION

1. Why is spiritual pride a temptation for Christians? What can we learn from the Publican?
2. Besides spiritual pride, what are some other Pharisee-like tendencies contemporary Christians are challenged by?
3. What are some different forms and ways we might encounter "least likely" persons in our lives?
4. What can we do for them? What can they teach us?
5. What are some ways that can increase our ability to see others the way Jesus sees them?

Bibliography

Buechner, Frederick, *Wishful Thinking* (Harper and Row, 1973)
———. *Peculiar Treasures* (Harper and Row, 1979)
Castle, Tony, comp., *The New Book of Christian Quotation* (Crossroad, 1988)
De Bertodano, Teresa, ed., *Daily Readings with Mother Teresa* (Harper and Row, 1993)
Dickens, Charles, *A Christmas Carol* (Bethany, 1999)
Goodhill, Ruth Marcus, ed., *The Wisdom of Heschel: Abraham Joshua Heschel* (Farrar, Straus, and Giroux, 1970)
Kushner, Harold, *When Bad Things Happen to Good People* (Schocken, 1981)
Lewis, C.S., *Mere Christianity* (MacMillan, 1952)
Maggio, Rosalie, comp., *Quotations for the Soul* (Prentice-Hall, 1997)
Martindale, Wane and Root, Jerry, eds., *The Quotable Lewis* (Tyndale House, 1989)
Woods, Ralph, comp., *The World Treasury of Religious Quotations* (Garland, 1966)

www.ingramcontent.com/pod-product-compliance
Lightning Source LLC
Chambersburg PA
CBHW071439160426
43195CB00013B/1964